THE GLOBALIST'S AGENDA
END GAME

CW00606803

Soul Esprit
Servant of the Lord Jesus Christ

NarrowGate Publishing

OTHER BOOKS BY SOUL ESPRIT

The Great Deception

The Coming of Wisdom

Seven Who Dared

The Criminal Fraternity

When Will the Illuminati Crash the Stock Market?

Fools Paradise

Genesis 1:29 Diet

Fractal Trading

Fractal Trading II

The Globalist's Agenda

Everything Is a Test

Book ordering: Barnes and Noble: bn.com
And other Online book sellers

All praise, honor, and glory be to God—
the LORD God Almighty, the Lord Jesus Christ

THE GLOBALIST'S AGENDA
END GAME

Corona Virus, 5G,
and the Fake Pandemic

———⊸∞∞⊸———

Soul Esprit
Servant of the Lord Jesus Christ

NarrowGate Publishing

The Globalist's Agenda End Game

Copyright © 2021 Soul Esprit

Published by NarrowGate Publishing

All Scripture verses quoted are from the Authorized 1611 King James Bible.

ISBN: 978-0-9841281-8-1

Library of Congress Control Number: 2013923573

For those who love the truth
and who are willing to die for The Truth

Contents

And he causeth all, both small and great, rich and poor, free and bond, to receive a mark in their right hand, or in their foreheads: And that no man might buy or sell, save he that had the mark, or the name of the beast, or the number of his name. . . . And the third angel followed them, saying with a loud voice, If any man worship the beast and his image, and receive his mark in his forehead, or in his hand, the same shall drink of the wine of the wrath of God, which is poured out without mixture into the cup of his indignation; and he shall be tormented with fire and brimstone in the presence of the holy angels, and in the presence of the Lamb: and the smoke of their torment ascendeth up for ever and ever: and they have no rest day nor night, who worship the beast and his image, and whosoever receiveth the mark of his name.

—Revelation 13:16,17; 14:9–11

Please note: This book is written from a higher perspective of Absolute Truth and thus does not conform to conventional thinking in terms of relative truth based upon any apparent reality. Assertions are directed toward a more comprehensive ordering of cause and effect, which may be unfamiliar to some readers.

PREFACE

The year 2020 marked the end of an era. It had previously been a time when government was somewhat bound by Constitutional principles and the providence of God rested upon America. Even though America, the Constitutional nation, ceased to exist in 1871 upon becoming an Illuminati chartered corporation, Washington DC yet continued to function as a political entity while serving the interests of its policy-dictating Illuminati overlords. (The "Illuminati" are a centralized banking cartel consisting of Luciferian-Satanist $multi-trillion generational crime families.) Then, in 1913, a second wound was struck at the heart of America when the European Rothschild banking dynasty established a central bank in the United States, which they termed the Federal Reserve. This entity was neither Federal nor a Reserve, but a privately-held corporation with a Board of Directors that are not U.S. citizens, and who are in the business of creating paper currency and loaning money at interest to the puppet regime in Washington DC. These loaned funds are used to operate federal business, such as meeting government employee payroll. The interest on the loaned funds is obtained by the collection of a personal income tax levied upon the people of America; an unConstitutional demand to extort wages from the working class. None of the annual confiscated tribute money is ever used to benefit the people from whom it was stolen. The citizens' extorted funds are used solely to finance the globalist's multifaceted Agenda.

The greatest country in the modern Western world continued on for another century through the oversight of a Shadow Government that orchestrated economic booms and busts, currency inflation and deflation, wars and recessions. Presidents were installed and deposed, and those who played along with the Globalist's Agenda were permitted to maintain the figurehead status of a world leader. Some did not comply, and Lincoln and the Kennedy's were summarily executed. Then, with the passage of the reign of Donald Trump, darkness quickly spread over the land, extinguishing any light from the world landscape that struggled to shine brightly, now dimmed by an overpowering evil. The consequences would be permanent and far-reaching.

During the 2020 election Joe Biden reportedly received more Electoral College votes than Donald Trump and became the successor to the U.S. Presidency. Biden had formerly been Vice President during the Obama Administration and was next in line to carry forward the globalist's commands for ushering in their long-awaited dictatorial world government. At that time it had seemed as if the hand of Almighty God delayed eventual Judgment when temporarily granting America a 4-year reprieve during Trump's single term of occupying the Oval Office. Yet, that was not the case, since a de-facto international banking cartel, as well as corporate interests, were behind the scenes arbitrators of DC politics. Like all U.S. "Presidents," Trump's supremacy as a leader was merely an illusion, his single-term tenure serving as the transition before God turned Americans over to their enemies and gave them up to destruction by the global Luciferian elites. Biden was chosen to be the facilitator for their End Game. The manipulated election results were controlled opposition to remove a capable leader and replace him with a senile puppet who would enact whatever legislative decrees his satanic Rothschild masters ordered him to perform. But Trump was also compromised.

In the manner of a Woodrow Wilson and all the U.S. figurehead Presidents since then (except JFK), Biden was a medium through which the unseen hand of the supra-government continued its briefly interrupted march toward the Revelation prophesy of a planet enslaved in a world dictatorship ruled by the second and third persons of the satanic trinity—the Antichrist (Global President) and False Prophet (Catholic Pope). Biden, an Illuminati shill with no affinity for Absolute Truth, or even relative truth, would go on to sign Legislation and Executive Orders to dismantle America and bring it into submission to the worldwide government of a future global President. The global vaccination program would be his major focus.

The globalists needed a false-flag event to bring in their New World Order dictatorial Fascist Police State, and an imaginary invisible virus was exactly the "enemy" for accommodating that purpose. Internationally, the fake pandemic Corona Virus vaccine became mandatory for everyone and was the people-control mechanism they were looking for in order to push forward their Globalist's Agenda.

A retrospective review of the present time would read like this:

'The devastating impact of the Biden Administration proved to be a sudden acceleration in the loss of freedom—not only because of mandatory forced vaccines—but also a myriad of other crimes against humanity. One of the first Constitutionally-guaranteed rights to fall was Freedom of Speech; suddenly it was a crime to tell the truth, and it was no longer permissible to speak out against fraudulent claims of a viral pandemic used by the world controllers as a pretense to create fear among the people and thereby control and enslave them to globalist totalitarian rule by receiving a Luciferase Biometric Quantum Dot Tattoo to validate they have been injected with a vaccine depopulation bioweapon.

At the time of the Biden takeover, foreign troops (Chinese) were reported at the U.S./Canadian border; video footage of long train cars carrying military tanks, armored transport vehicles and other equipment and weapons, presumably for deployment against the North American citizenry who protest or refuse to be administered the C–19 vaccine. (FEMA camps had years previously been constructed throughout America to incarcerate large numbers of vaccine protestors and those who would not submit to curfews, business closures, lockdown home quarantines, and other restrictions.)

The right to gun ownership was the next Constitutional freedom to be extinguished, and confiscation of all firearms was achieved via door to door searches and seizures by mercenary defected local police, U.S. military and invading Chinese army. In the manner of the Hegelian Dialect, Trump had been "Pro Gun," and that was a "problem" for his globalist masters seeking total control and no possibility among the sheep-like people for an uprising by force to recover their lost God-given freedoms.

In past history, the only effective means to resist tyrannical government was by the exercise of deadly force; guns have always been integral for retaining independence from oppressive governments. This is not sedition, but a Constitutional right, as stated by one of America's key founding fathers, Thomas Jefferson, who, in the Declaration of Independence, stated: "Whenever any form of government becomes destructive of these ends, it is the right of the people to alter or to abolish it, and to institute a new government, laying its foundation on such principles, and organizing its powers in such form, as to them shall seem most likely to effect their safety and happiness." Historically, tyrannical rulership has never been removed by negotiations, but was always deposed by a small minority of citizens who replaced defective leaders by means of violent overthrow. Without guns, or some form of superior weaponry, that is not possible.

Once guns were taken out of the hands of the citizenry and retained in the hands of the legal criminal element—government—there was nothing to stop the psychopaths in power from quickly advancing toward a worldwide dictatorship. A loss of guns directly resulted in a global takeover as the one percent righteous were unable to stage resistance to the pervasive tyranny kicking in their front door.

Daily fabricated news of hospitalizations and deaths falsely attributed to Corona Virus continued to rise as the diagnostic criteria included every possibility of death to be assigned to the imaginary virus. Testing positive for "Corona Virus" was a near certainty because of a broad spectrum of blood-borne indicators—all present in healthy individuals—and any one of which "confirmed" the presence of the invisible Covid deception. Disinformation claiming a rising pandemic death toll and more vaccines to control viral "Variants" were a weekly media announcement for maintaining the world's people in a constant state of apprehension and irrational fear.

A Covid ID Certificate was required of every global citizen in order to prove they had been vaccinated, and a scannable fingerprint micro-dot luminescent tattoo was embedded in their index finger, back of the right hand, or forehead of all those who eagerly stood in line to receive the mandatory identification. The C–19 vaccine contained a nano-sized computer chip that crossed the blood-brain barrier to lodge in the frontal lobe of the Cerebral Cortex, and thus confirmed a 2000 year old prophesy (Revelation 13:16,17) foretelling of a mysterious Mark in the forehead or hand; no one was able to buy or sell without damning their soul to hell. Food rationing soon followed, and without proof of having been vaccinated for the nonexistent Covid, people were denied service at commercial food sources, including supermarkets, grocery stores, and restaurants. Without proof of vaccination one was prohibited from holding a job, transacting business, and engaging in any form of commerce. In every city and town there were dejected citizens wandering the streets in search of food. Dumpsters were chained and locked to prevent scavaging by the many starving recently homeless who managed to escape unlawful arrest because they would not submit to the soul-damning vaccine Mark of the Beast. Citizen tracking made possible by the embedded Covid vaccine microchip (Contact Tracing) was the globalist's assurance that the vaccination status of every person on earth (7.5 billion) could instantaneously be ascertained, and their whereabouts, and the exact location of those who did not comply with being quarantined in their homes could be determined with great precision. (The government demand for "Social Distancing" of 6 feet has nothing to do with preventing the spead of a nonexistent Corona Virus, but is intended to eliminate false readings created by people standing close together or in groups, which, on satellite imaging appears as a single individual and provides an inaccurate "body count.")

Retail closures and lockdown home quarantines were declared whenever the world controllers desired the citizenry to remain in constant proximity to a television set in order to be administered yet another dose of mind-control fake news designed to reinforce previously conditioned programmed behavior suitable for servile slaves. While sequestered in their homes—with loss of job and unable to communicate with others and therefore organize against the oppressive tyranny—they were fed a daily diet of New World Order misinformation and disinformation, intelligence-insulting falsehoods, and simplistic phrases to perpetuate the lie. "Stay Safe," "We're in this together," and the "New Normal" were globalist mantras parroted by the reduced IQ vaccinated populous who believed the Covid falsehood and uncritically adopted the motivational slogans into their lexicon. Having effectively lost the ability to think independently of TV *programming*, they proved to be devoid of any higher cognitive faculty that would have otherwise enabled them to see through the globalist's staged theater. Political propaganda blared from their TV's and computer monitors 24/7 to maintain them in an altered state of hypnotic subconsciousness for absorbing subliminal and verbal suggestions that neutralized or erased any original thought, righteous indignation, and the testosterone to stand up to tyranny. Stripped of their manhood and humanity, they could only mindlessly obey their oppressors and parrot simplistic clichés with uncanny consistency.

The worldwide closing of public facilities, schools, businesses, restaurants and other social venues were integral to the Globalist's Agenda for sustaining the level of people-control necessary to elicit a predictable trauma-conditioned fear response among the citizenry. Instantly, the entire world population was transformed into robotized unthinking zombies lacking any noble virtue or aspirations other than to obey a virtual government run behind the scenes by a Luciferian cabal under the direction of the chief fallen angel, Lucifer/Satan. Because of their rejection of the truth and their disdain for righteousness, God sent them a curse that condemned them to an eternity of darkness; without light, without reason, without hope, and without the truth of God Jesus Christ. Second Thessalonians 2:10–12: *And with all deceivableness of unrighteousness in them that*

perish: because they received not the love of the truth, that they might be
saved. And for this cause God shall sent them strong delusion, that they
should believe a lie: that they all might be damned who believed not
the truth, but had pleasure in unrighteousness. (i.e. Hell is the certain
destination for all those many who believed Satan's fake pandemic
lie and submitted to his Revelation 13:16 Mark of the Beast Covid
vaccine 666 microchip.) In the end, the only people who survived
the just wrath of God were the very few who resisted a satanic government—all the way to the end of their life—having died martyrs
when arrested, incarcerated, tortured and killed.'

The Biden Administration is pro-Luciferian and therefore consid-
ers Christians to be "terrorists." Like an aging demented lap dog,
he will obey his Illuminati handlers and use the pretense of a fake
pandemic to force compliance and to silence the few righteous who
boldly stand up and proclaim the truth about the Covid deception.
These extraordinary people love the truth, and their actions are a
manifestation of their love for God Jesus Christ, who is *The Truth*:
John 14:6: "*I am the way, the truth, and the life.*" Like Barack Obama,
Biden hates the living God and will act on orders from his Illuminati handlers to arrest, imprison, and exterminate all witness to that
most High name. "Truth-tellers" who expose the Covid deception
behind the fabricated pandemic will be branded by the controlled
media and ostracized by the mind-controlled dumbed-down masses.
Many of those who proclaim the truth will ultimately be taken to
"Re-education Centers" (FEMA Death Camps) and will have to sacrifice their life for The Truth. At the start of the Biden reign of terror,
religious persecution in America has finally arrived.

INTRODUCTION

Corona Virus is listed in the Medline Plus Medical Encyclopedia as the causal agent for *the Common Cold*. The globalist's depopulation agenda is a fake pandemic attributed to Corona Virus, which, technically, does not exist (i.e. the character and action of the biological vector bears no resemblance to the controlled media cover story). Claims of a global infectious disease are a fabricated scenario used as a pretense to elicit fear among the world population. What better way to control the world's people than by terrorizing them with irrational fear? When a person is fearful, that individual will modify their behavior to avoid the perceived negative consequences which the fear evokes. When a group of people, or a nation, or the entire world has been made fearful, those few orchestrating the fear response will have total control over the behavior of the targeted population, and the people will do whatever is demanded of them. The globalists realize they can use fear as an effective tool to elict any kind of reaction, and that the fear response does not require an actual cause for the fear, but only the perception of something to be feared. This is exactly what they did in the case of Corona Virus when lying to create a Covid media campaign to justify a nonexistent pandemic with the consequent need for people everywhere to be fearful and at the same time follow criminal government decrees, dictates, and commands. In terms of an inappropriate fear response, there is no "deadly Corona Virus" to be afraid of, and therefore the unConstitutional government-mandated medical orders to wear a mask, maintain social distance, and submit to a vaccine serves an ulterior motive. That motive is the Globalist's Agenda to control or eradicate by vaccine injection, incarceration, or by force, large numbers of the human population.

There is no nongovernment-funded science to support the vaccine theory as a safe and effective public health measure. Vaccines are often the cause of the disease they purport to protect the individual from acquiring. (e.g. Nearly all known cases of Polio were caused by the Polio Vaccine.) Graphs illustrating a timeline for the administration of a vaccine versus the eradication of a disease all show there exists no direct correlation between vaccine programs and disease eradication. The data clearly demonstrates that the disease was already in an advanced state of remission at the time of commencement of a vaccine campaign. Censoring this null correlation from being reported to the public is how the globalist's medical crime cartel are enabled to offer their own fraudulent research and testing as "proof" of vaccine efficacy.

Historically, no public health vaccination programs have been demonstrated to be effective for the eradication of infectious disease; in every case the causal factor for control or elimination of a disease such as Smallpox, Malaria, Colera, Yellow Fever, etc, was improved sanitation, better nutrition, heathier living conditions. False claims made by the medical crime community are based upon epidemiological studies which produce notoriously ambiguous and erronous data that can be manipulated and interpreted to accomodate any desired outcome which serves the purpose of the power-wielding faction.

There are no independent scientific studies—which are not funded by government—proving that the globalist's presumed Covid viral agent is capable of causing death among the world population. Thus, the globalist's stated need for a vaccine is shown to be entirely false, fabricated, unnecessary, and a crime against humanity. As this book will make obvious to any rational person, their expressed urgency to vaccinate everyone is a genocidal motivation to inoculate with disease, microchip, trace/track, and splice nonhuman DNA into every person on earth. The Covid vaccine ruse is the Hegelian Dialectic which has worked so well in the past to change the cultural paradigm for bringing about a desired result: Create a "virus problem," offer the "vaccine solution," reduce the global population, change human genetics, enslave the people of the world in an Orwellian control grid. It worked for the 911 lie; it is working and will continue to work for the fake Corona Virus Pandemic lie. The weaponized Covid vaccine is integral to the success of the world controllers' media-driven fear-mongering manufactured pandemic. With the world population forced to submit to a trace and track bioweapon vaccine, the Globalist's Agenda End Game will be a fait accompli.

Corona Virus is history's greatest hoax. Eugenicist and serial killer Bill Gates owns the patent (application submitted in 2015; granted in 2018) for this 2019 laboratory-created strain of Influenza, the *Common Flu*. The fabricated pandemic fear is a deception of the greatest magnitude and has been planned by the Luciferian globalists in advance of the staged outbreak in 2019. It is heavily promoted by their controlled media to force the world masses to believe and comply with the Covid comic farce, with the ultimate objective of a totalitarian worldwide government. This cannot be achieved until the globalists have established total control over every person's life, to the extent that no one retains a Free Will for making conscious rational decisions. Repeatedly traumatized by fake news and official proclamations designed to induce irrational fear, periodically injected with yet another vaccine biowarfare agent, the world's people grovel at the feet of billionaire psychopaths laughing hysterically at the sheer gullibility and lack of moral character of the people to rise up and oppose a planned falsehood of international dimensions.

The Corona Virus vaccine contains biological components that will alter human genetics, and a programmable nano-sized microchip that will enable the creation of a global "Hive Mind" by 5G cell towers and Starlink satellite electromagnetic frequency transmissions. The injected mRNA is bioengineered to direct gene splicing for altering DNA from human to nonhuman. Those who receive any of the "pandemic vaccines" will have programmable nanorobots in their body which will exacerbate their ability to think independently of the globalist's design. Consequently, with the Corona Virus vaccine, human freedom will no longer be either free or human.

The creation of a deception to the degree of the fake Corona Virus Pandemic required attacking the world populous in several key areas, most significantly the loss of ability to discern truth from falsehood. The Rothschild's owned and controlled global media has previously been successful in maintaining a level of ignorance, reduced cognitive engagement, and heightened fear among the undiscerning world masses who, for decades, have been mind-controlled by the TV to only believe what they hear and see on the broadcasted fake news and predictive Hollywood films. People all over the world are psychologically conditioned by entertainment, sporting events, and valueless television "programming" which contributes nothing to the development of critical thinking skills and the exercise of rational judgment. Over the course of several decades the poisoning of the food, water, and air—in combination with weaponized vaccines—has resulted in diminished cognitive capability among the citizenry, such that the mass majority have been transformed into sheep-like obeisance to their invisible controlling masters. Lacking discernment for piercing through the veil of the media deception, fear and deceit is all they know; truth and the propensity to think on their own is foreign to them and is no longer an option. They have been mind-controlled by the television, the fake news, the Google-censored truth, and can therefore only "know" what their controllers want them to know. In the process they have become unwitting pawns blinded to the voice of reason, unable to discern deceit from veracity. This is not only a consequence of concerted mind-control and media censorship, but is also a spiritual curse sent from God in response to their recalcitrant rejection and contempt for the truth. Once more, the explanation for why this has occurred is Second Thessalonians 2:10,11: *And with all deceivableness of unrighteousness in them that perish; because they received not the love of the truth, that they might be saved. And for this cause God shall send them strong delusion, that they should believe a lie.* Their rejection and contempt for the truth is actually a reflection of their rejection and contempt for God Jesus Christ, who stated in

John 14:6: *I am the way, the truth, and the life: no man cometh unto the Father, but by me.* And the consequence is: . . . *That they all might be damned who believed not the truth, but had pleasure in unrighteousness (v.12).* The ultimate result of having rejected the truth and believing a pernicious lie such as the Corona Virus fake pandemic is eternal soul damnation in the Lake of Fire. Revelation 14:9–11: *And the third angel followed them, saying with a loud voice, If any man worship the beast and his image, and receive his mark in his forehead, or in his hand, The same shall drink of the wine of the wrath of God, which is poured out without mixture into the cup of his indignation; and he shall be tormented with fire and brimstone in the presence of the holy angels, and in the presence of the Lamb:And the smoke of their torment ascendeth up for ever and ever: and they have no rest day nor night, who worship the beast and his image, and whosoever receiveth the mark of his name.*

Here is what will happen to those who refuse the Covid vaccine or any other fake pandemic vaccine:

- Cannot buy or sell (Rev 13:16,17).

- Indefinite home quarantine or incarceration in FEMA Detention Camps.

- Confiscation of all assets.

- Cut off from participating in commerce and functioning in open society.

This will mean job loss, poverty, social isolation, homelessness, starvation.

Here is what will happen to those who submit to the vaccine:

- Inoculation of toxic elements: Mercury, Aluminum, Lead, Arsenic; technological components such as nanorobots and other foreign matter such as fetal tissue and live cancer cells.

- Microchip tracking everywhere on the planet.

- Nonhuman DNA spliced into chromosomes (no longer human).

- Take-over of natural immunity by mRNA bioengineered gene sequencing that codes for the lethal virus.

- Global mind-link with Neuralink via 5G towers and Starlink satellites.

This will mean total loss of libery, loss of Free Will and the ability to choose, loss of soul for eternity in the Lake of Fire (Revelation 14:9–11).

Conclusion: From both temporal and eternal considerations, it is in one's best interest not to submit to any vaccines, and especially the weaponized Corona Virus and subsequent fake pandemic "variant" vaccines.

"It is difficult to free fools from the chains they revere."
—Voltaire

"None are more hopelessly enslaved
than those who falsely believe they are free."
—Johann Wolfgang Von Goethe

CHAPTER 1

AS IT WAS
IN THE DAYS OF NOAH

But as the days of Noah were, so shall also the coming of the Son of man be.   —Matthew 25:37

The complete story of mankind's future destiny has already been written in the Noah account. The reason why God flooded the earth at that time and destroyed everyone except Noah and his family (total of 8), is because human genetics were corrupted by human-demon hybrids (Nephilim), and even the animals were part of the genomic alteration. So, God started over again. Presently, in today's modern world, we have the same occurrence. Read Genesis 6, verse 4 and you will see that these human-demons are back, and they are Bill Gates, Elon Musk, Jared Kushner, Rothschilds, Rockefellers, Windsors, Joe Biden, Barack Obama, Clintons, Bushes, George Soros, and thousands of others. Genesis 6:4, KJV: *There were giants in the earth in those days; and also after that, when the sons of God came in unto the daughters of men, and they bare children to them, the same became mighty men which were of old, men of renown.*

During the time of Noah, God destroyed mankind because of Nephilim genetic contamination. Today, it is bioweaponized vaccines with CrispR gene-splicing capability that will be the cause of his wrath and the end of this present Age. The fake pandemic Corona Virus vaccine (and all subsequent vaccines) is the means by which the Nephilim hybrid globalists will splice gene instructions into human DNA to suppress the immune response and replicate vaccine-injected viruses that will kill the human host. By means of vaccines they will transcribe nonhuman DNA to once more corrupt man's genetics. Consequently, God will again wipe out most of mankind, and he will do it by a combination of factors, including the Covid and SPARS vaccines, natural disasters (e.g. asteroid collision with Earth); and, for the Saved, government genocide via induced starvation, police murders, FEMA Detention, Concentration Camp beheadings. There is no escaping this conclusion, for Bible prophesy tells of its inevitability (Daniel 7:25, Matthew 24, Luke 21, Revelation 6:9). The key point is that the purpose of the fake pandemic vaccines is to drastically reduce the global population and change human genetics into nonhuman genetics, link the global Hive Mind to the AI WiFi Starlink control grid (thereby replacing Free Will with Artificial Intelligence), and thus use nanotechnology to change the image of man into the image of Lucifer/Satan. At that point God will intervene and conclude the present phase of mankind.

The Luciferian globalists are attempting to use vaccine nanotechnology to obliterate human Free Will and radically alter human genes by corruption with nonhuman genes, which is the same reason why, 6,000 years ago, God destroyed all the inhabitants of the earth, except for Noah and his family. The unfolding future scenario for the fulfillment of this Bible prophesy is as follows:

- 2019: December 21, Winter Solstice/Satanic holiday: Enactment of scripted scenario of a viral agent used as justification for the false claim of a pandemic to warrant a worldwide shutdown.

- 2020: Roll out of media-driven Covid fake pandemic; utilization of social restrictions under the pretense of "virus control" and as a means of conditioning the global population for the coming "people control."

- 2021: Widespread availability of weaponized Covid vaccines to trace and track everyone on the planet and change human genetics.

January: Covid biowarfare vaccine distributed in Europe and to select health care workers and demographic groups (e.g. over 75).

June: Covid biowarfare vaccine available to general public; injection of the first part of a two-part bioweapon: neurological toxins, microchip, gene-splicing DNA, and enabled for neural linkage to the AI satellite control grid. (Nearly everyone will gratefully stand in line to receive the vaccine death shot, believing it will "protect" them from "Corona Virus" and "stop the Covid Pandemic.")

September: Covid biowarfare vaccine mandatory; arrest/jail/forced vaccination for those many who will refuse and resist. Required "Proof of Vaccination" digital ID Certificate. Civil unrest, protest, rioting.

- 2022: Top in the U.S. and world financial markets.

- 2022–2025/2027: Stages in Crash of the U.S. and world economies; Dollar currency replaced by cashless digital currency.

- 2025–2028: Planned second fake pandemic: "SPARS"—"Variants" requiring more vaccines, quarantines, lockdowns, school closures, business shutdowns, etc. Luminescent biometric quantum dot tattoo branded onto back of right hand or forehead.

- 2030: Agenda 2030; all elements of Luciferian New World Order in place and ready for implementation; people-control grid operational and ready for deployment. The human brain "Hive Mind" connected to Artificial Intelligence. A Dystopian society, Communism/Socialism/Fascism.

- 2030–2050: The last generation. "Hell on earth"—Satan's kingdom rules over the masses of the lost and deceived. Global chaos. The Bible states in Matthew 24:22 that Satan would kill everyone if Jesus didn't return by this time: *And except those days should be shortened, there should no flesh be saved: but for the elect's sake those days shall be shortened.*

- 2051: End of the present Age of mankind. Return of Jesus Christ (ref. Appendix B).

The Globalist's Agenda End Game is a process of culling humanity, yet there is another "Culling" simultaneously taking place at this time in human history. In a spiritual sense it involves, not the temporal body, but the eternal soul, for God is using the fake pandemic as a means to prove who will acknowledge the lie and reject the truth. There is "planned destruction," but it is not death by wars, as in the past; nor is it by infanticide, as practiced by ancient cultures and today's abortion clinics. It is death *by vaccination*, by forced vaccines administered under the pretense of a nonexistent disease pandemic. And, what is more, it is death of the human soul by steadfast rejection of The Truth, Jesus Christ.

CHAPTER 2

THE GREAT RESET: CORONA VIRUS FAKE PANDEMIC— A PRETENSE FOR WORLD GOVERNMENT

"Anti-vaxxers"
"We're all in this together, apart."
"Be Safe."
—Media-promoted globalist mantras

The above catch phrases were invented by the globalist's and circulated by their controlled media as an appeal to irrational minds for excluding evidences which argue against the persistent claims by the controlled news for the existence of a deadly contagious virus. Simplistic slogans serve the agenda of the globalists by inducing among the world's people a sense of fear, comradarie, and group solidarity that seeks a savior to rescue them from a dreaded invisible enemy. A universal consensus is continually reinforced by everyday contact with throngs of mind-controlled subservient slaves wearing a face diaper (mask) and shunning close contact with those in proximity. All over the world the "Sheeple" march in lock-step to what, for a rational person, is a painfully obvious and laughable hoax.

The sheep-like compliance of the world masses in response to the globalist's outcry of a pandemic is typified by the American people who uncritically accept whatever the controlled media programs

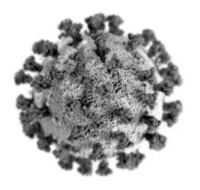

Corona Virus presumed lethal vector utilized by the globalists to justify ushering in their totalitarian world government. On the basis of one massive deception the population of the world has become enslaved to the Globalist's Agenda End Game.

them to believe. They saw it on TV, so it must be true, they think. They cannot even conceive that there is no rational basis for believing that a Corona Virus pandemic exists, and they are incapable of rising up in protest, or at least shouting, "It's not about virus control, it's about people control!" Uninformed, and lacking any apparent interest in discovering the truth, virtually no one—in a world population of some 7.5 billion people—has voiced the observation that "The Emperor isn't wearing a beautiful robe." Instead, they smile placidly while going about their daily routine, never suspecting that they are about to become a sacrificial offering to the globalist's master—Lucifer/Satan.

OPERATION WARP SPEED

Operation Warp Speed is the full roll out of the Covid vaccine first developed by BioNTech/Pfizer and Moderna. This directive was promoted by Donald Trump during his last days of office, and who hired serial killer eugenicist, Bill Gates, to expedite the global genocide vaccine program. Therefore, appearances to the contrary, Trump capitulated to the demands of his Illuminati crime family/ supra-government handlers. (Perhaps he realized he had no other choice because they would assassinate him if he refused.) The incumbent to the Oval Office, Joe Biden, will accelerate fake pandemic propaganda and promote global genocide Covid vaccinations still further.

A key aspect of the End Game is to connect the human brain to Artificial Intelligence via Neuralink by the year 2030. The person chosen by the Illuminati to run Operation Warp Speed, Moncef Slaoui, is an expert on injectable brain-machine interface, and was formerly the head researcher at GlaxoSmithKline, a British multinational pharmaceutical company. He will also direct the Neuralink hook up of the mind of every human being on the planet to the Hive Mind SpaceX Starlink 5G WiFi surveillance control grid. Administration of a microchip-directed CrispR gene-splicing vaccine via COVID and SPARS hypodermic injection is the essential intermediate step for accomplishing that goal.

The Rothschild's supra-government mass media has been very effective in mind-controlling and programming the global population into acceptance of the Covid disinformation official narrative which enables them to induce billions of people to comply with senseless government decrees (wear a mask, practice social distancing, get vaccinated), and submit to ongoing sanitation/disinfectation proceedures, curtailment of social interactions, lock-down quarantines, and school/business closures, on demand. The attainment of worldwide tyranny cannot proceed without weaponized genocidal vaccinations that can be utilized as a pretense to enable global tracking, alteration of human genetics, brain interface with Artifical Intelligence, and mass genocide. The microchip in the vaccine is a nanodot and programmable to direct gene-splicing (CrispR) by adding and deleting DNA gene sequences. (The Covid vaccine is a messenger RNA delivery system that substitutes bioengineered altered genes for protein sequences from DNA to encode every cell in the human body with nonhuman genetics.) The dire consequences consist of induced diseases and serious bodily reactions like anaphalatic shock, skin eruptions, cardiac arrest and lethal systemic infection. The Bible forewarned of this, and today the nanotechnology exists to genetically change humans into nonhumans; transforming the image of the living God into the transhuman image of a non-living Satan. This is being expedited by the globalists who are elated that their millenial plan has finally been unveiled and is moving forward at warp speed.

COVID = COVID VACCINE ID

An injectable *bioweapon* is the ultimate tracking and behavior control mechanism. The vaccine microchip component is utilized by the globalist world controllers for ID verification and stores personal and financial information that can be turned on or off to reward or punish the recipient, thus controlling behavior of the injectee by preventing access to financial resources and vital information needed for survival. The gene-splicing capability will rewrite human DNA sequencing to create never before seen strains of nonhuman subspecies. Neuralink human–to–computer interface will become a reality upon global vaccinations and a sufficient number of Starlink surveillance satellites beaming 5G frequencies to earth. In the new cashless digital 666 human control system, financial transactions will no longer be mediated by paper currency, but rather by digital noncurrency electronic credits and debits. After the planned collapse of the global economy, the currency will not be paper or gold, but a type of cashless crypto-currency, like Bitcoin, except that it will be controlled by the world government. (Crypto-currencies are a ponzi scheme where value is determined by whatever investors perceive it to be; the global cashless currency shall be subject to the determination of the world controllers who manipulate that perception to their own advantage.) In the subsequent phase of human social and biological engineering, digital currency will be combined with digital identification and tracking. This will be accomplished by a debit and credit card system transferred directly into the physical body by means of a vaccine injection. Using the ruse of a fake pandemic, personal ID and tracking, financial accounting, and downloadable nanotechnological components will become incorporated into human beings.

Corona Virus is the new 911 of staged terrorism. Implemented by governments worldwide, the Covid fake pandemic is a smoke screen to start global government. The end result is the creation of a planetary-wide surveillance control grid, digital identification, global tracking, genetic alteration, and the linkage of the human brain with quantum computers. A microchip vaccine, or a series of vaccines, will enable human hookup to the global financial system for maximum people control.

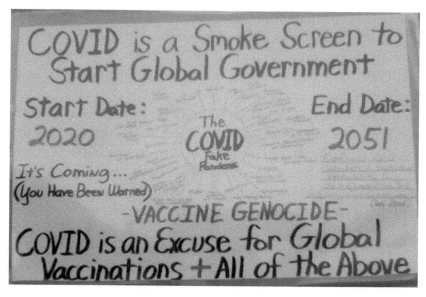

The Covid fake pandemic is a smoke screen for establishing the globalist's long awaited New World Order Luciferian Society built on fear and violence, brainwashing and mind-control, propaganda and lies, eugenics and dehumanization, sterilization and disinfectation.

An imaginary "Corona Virus" is the impetus for the so-called Great Reset proposed by the World Economic Forum, and involves a list of criteria which comprise the Globalist's Agenda. Preventing people from gathering together in groups to inhibit their power to protest and resist, and business shutdowns and lockdown home quarantines under the guise of protecting everyone from a nonexistent pandemic, are only the beginning of the greatest political sabotage the world has ever known. The globalist's proposal is to pay people to stay at home (Stimulus Checks), preventing them from organizing into groups that could lead to citizen revolt and action taken against government tyranny and restrictions imposed under the pretense of a pandemic.

Home lockdowns, no travel permitted, temperature checked by souless government human drones, slow kill depopulation, economic devastation, list of resisters for termination, loss of free speech, gun confiscation/prohibition of ammunition purchases, families separated, FEMA incarceration and hydraulic guillotines—from the present time onward, the future of mankind will be characterized by escalating terror designed for enslavement by a worldwide Communist/Socialist/Facist government of unprecedented tyranny and injustice.

There exists many subcategories and minor agendas which enable the larger Corona Virus Fake Pandemic Agenda. The Covid deception can only become entrenched in an individual's life if the Truth of God Jesus Christ is not the central focus. When a love for The Truth (God Jesus Christ) has been replaced by a love for Satan's religion (man's government), the mind and body easily follows, and people become *sheeple*.

The following is a list of some of the more prevalent means by which the globalists will accomplish their "Great Reset" for attaining worldwide dictatorial control of the human sheeple population:

- Agenda 21

- Agenda 2030

- Digital ID 2020

- Covid Vaccine Fingerprint Scan

- Cashless World Society

- Microdot Luciferase tattoo in back of right hand or forehead

- Fake News

- Fake Science

- Forced Vaccines

- Never-ending series of pandemics requiring more restrictions and more vaccines ("Variants") ref. predictive programming Hollywood film, "Songbird," schedule for release end of 2021

- Complicit Hospitals/Clinics, Doctors, Nurses, Healthcare workers, and Government Agencies

- UN Population Control Organizations: World Health Organization, Center for Disease Control, World Economic Forum, etc.

- Vaccine-injectable Microchips

- DNA Splicing (mRNA/gene insertion/deletion)

- 5G WiFi via Starlink Satellites and 5G towers: virus creation

- 50,000 global satellite surveillance

- Curfews and Home Quarantines

- Neuralink-Human Computer Interface (Transhumanism) 5G connection of human minds (Hive Mind) to Artificial Intelligence (AI)

- School Closings

- Closings of Public Facilities (Libraries, Community Gatherings, etc.)

- Business Closings (Corporations, Small Businesses, Restaurants, etc.)

- Business Failures

- Bank failures and Stock Market Crash (U.S. and Global)

- Use of Police and Military to Force Vaccine Compliance (HR 6666)

- FEMA Detention Centers (Death Camps) for resisters

- Chemtrails: artificial clouds, nano-particulate air, electrified atmosphere; human body as an electro-conductive receiver

- HAARP (High Altitude Active Auroral Research Project) microwave frequency generator, Chemtrail interface, weather modification, creation of natural disasters, human mind control

Covid was planned far in advance as a means to invade the human body with nanotechnological components via mandatory vaccinations. Genocidal alpha globalist, Bill Gates, has assumed a prominent role in funding and promoting *biowarfare* vaccines as a means to significantly reduce the world population and enable control of all the inhabitants of the earth; his ultimate objective is to download an AI operating system into everyone in the world. Just as his Microsoft company installed an operating system into PC's, he has extended that concept to installing an operating system into living human bodies. By the pretense of fake pandemic vaccines, he will install into humans "viruses" to create a "human operating system" with regular mind-control programming "updates." His actions are not humanitarian, but genocidal. As Robert Kennedy, Jr, a vaccine injury lawyer, has noted, "Vaccines, for Bill Gates, are a strategic philanthropy that feed his many vaccine-related businesses and give him dictatorial control over global health policy. Gates' obsession with vaccines seems fueled by a messanic conviction that he is ordained to save the world with technology and a god-like willingness to experiment [and sacrifice] the lives of lesser humans." But Kennedy's observation only scratches the surface of a much more diabolical and ambitious project that will significantly reduce the global population, change the genome from human to nonhuman, and reduce human consciousness and Free Will to the status of a programmable computer operating system.

The FDA, CDC, and "Big Pharma" are media-promoted by "Big Tech" Internet gate-keepers Google, YouTube, Facebook and Instagram, in support of their plan to maim and kill billions of people by means of a bioengineered technoweapon and experimental high-fatality drug—the Corona Virus vaccine and all subsequent vaccines—which have not been tested upon humans in any nongovernment-funded double-blind clinical studies. The vaccines have been revealed by insiders to alter human genetics, and through programmable nanotechnology cognitively rewire, disable, or kill off large numbers of humanity. The experimental Covid vaccines have not been proven to be safe or effective for human usage. The globalists did not intend them for prevention of disease, but rather as a means of genocide, mind-control, and genetic alteration. The microdot chip component will identify and track the recipient; the CrispR gene-splicing component is bioengineered into the vaccine-injected mRNA to delete and insert foreign genetic material into chromosomal DNA; signals from SpaceX Starlink satellites and 5G towers will transmit an ongoing stream of human-control programming for the vaccine-injected microchip that will link the planetary Hive Mind to AI quantum supercomputers.

THE GREAT VACCINE HOAX

When the normal antigen/antibody immune response has been replaced by "gene-spliced vaccine immunity" the body loses its ability to defend against subsequent viral or bacterial invasions. Instead of *attacking and killing* invading pathogens, the re-programmed immune system *reproduces* it. Through a breakdown of natural immunity, the proliferation of pathogens via sabotaged DNA replication results in the body's total dependency upon further gene-splicing vaccines, as the body's normal immune response to disease has been disabled and is no longer functional.

For more than a century, vaccine-induced *brain inflamation* has been known as a side effect of an injection by vaccine antigens, and manifests as a screaming infant, psychotic killer teen, or depressed suicidal elderly—all victims of a massive conspiracy to depopulate and make cognitively unfit the whole of humanity. While the sold-out perpetrators are complicit in the genocide by claiming that vaccines are safe, effective, harmless, and confer protection, the public's health is seriously compromised as increasingly more people become ill, disabled, or dead as a direct consequence of being stabbed with a hypodermic needle.

The human brain is under attack whenever a vaccine has been injected into the body. Immediately upon birth, an infant is seized by hospital staff and inoculated with Hepatitis B vaccine, a concoction of ingredients that will cause life-long irreversible neurological damage. Newborn infants sometime instantly experience anaphalactic shock, seizure, convulsions, and either death or permanent brain tissue destruction. Of further critical importance in this regard is the fact that infants do not contract Hepatitis B; only IV drug users and prostitutes contract Hepatitis B. So, why is the infant being injected?

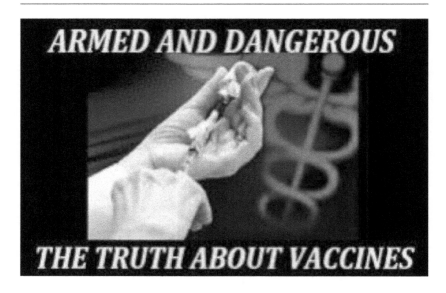

The chemical constituents of a vaccine shot are lethal to a human being, and especially for an infant or a child, due to an unformed immune system and the proportion of body weight to the concentration of toxins. Among the list of vaccine ingredients are Mercury (Methylmercury/Thimerosal, a preservative of the aqueous mixture), Aluminum, Lead, Arsenic, and other chemical elements, some that are the most lethal on the planet. The Mercury content of vaccines was not reduced or eliminated—as proposed in 1999 by the Public Health Service agencies, the American Academy of Pediatrics, and vaccine manufacturers—but instead, it was *increased*! (They lied.) Animal fetal tissue, parts of the pathogen being inoculated against, and other foreign matter constitute a witch's brew that is so dangerous to humans that few can survive it without some form of physical malady or cognitive dysfunction. For an infant or young child that has not yet fully developed an immune system, there often results any combination of symptoms, including Aspergers Syndrome, Autism, learning disabilities, psychological problems, social behavioral dysfunction, and various other forms of cognitive deficit. From 1980 to the present, the rate of Autism in children has increased from 1 in 10,000, to 1 in 28, and that figure is rapidly accelerating.

Today, one out of every 6 children has a learning disability; teenage psychosis and suicide is presently rampant. There is an established provable link between the administration of a vaccine and adverse symptomologies. A direct correlation exists between the time an infant, child, or an adult is subjected to vaccine toxins, and the immediate or delayed onset of physical or cognitive repercussions, which are typically attributed to an "unknown" cause. The doctor, pharmaceutical companies, hospitals and health clinics are all protected from vaccine damage accountability by the 2005 Public Readiness and Emergency Preparedness Act (PREPA or the PREP Act) which insures corporate freedoms from liability.

The vaccine assault upon infants and children represents an accumulation of biowarfare agents specifically designed to cause disability or death. The administration of vaccines is tantamount to premeditated murder and is a crime against humanity. According to Dr. Sherri Tenpenny, the following is a typical scenario:

> As if starting life by being stabbed and injected with chemicals isn't horrifying enough, around the 60 day of life, infants are subjected to more stabbing and injecting: DTaP, HiB, polio, Prevnar 13, a second dose of hepatitis B and a squirt of oral rotavirus vaccine.
>
> According to the US pediatric schedule, this onslaught is repeated twice, every 60 days. In all, 95 viral or bacterial antigens and measurable amounts of a dozen different chemicals are deposited into an infant by six months of age. By five years of age, a fully vaccinated, forty-pound human will have received 35 injections, containing at least 110 different weakened pathogens (or pathogen particles), and an assortment of 59 different chemicals. The little tot will also be contaminated [with] foreign proteins: stray viral DNA, four types of animal cells, cells from aborted fetal tissue and bits of human albumin. How children survive these aggressive attacks is a testament to the resilience of the human body. But what impact does this toxic foreign matter have on the rapidly developing brain? No one really knows and no one is looking.

Yet, there are people who do know what the consequences of vaccines are, especially for young children. One of them is Dr. Russel Blaylock, a world renoun neurosurgeon who has studied the effects which vaccinations have upon the human brain. Conducting his own nongovernment-funded research, his conclusions are succinctly summarized: https://www.talkingaboutthescience.com/studies/Blaylock-openarticle.pdf. The following is an excerpt:

The Compelling Link Between Autism and the Vaccination Program: There are over one million children, and even adults, with Autism and the numbers continue to grow. This is a medical disaster of monumental proportions.

The link to the vaccine program is scientifically and logically compelling but these same medical elitists refuse to listen.

In 1983, before the Autism epidemic began, children received 10 vaccinations before attending school, and the Autism incidence was 1 in 10,000. Today they are receiving 24 vaccines before 1 year, and 36 by the time they attend school, and the Autism is now 1 in 150 births. [This is a dated statistic; the actual current rate (2020) is even lower than the reported 1 in 28.]

Medical "experts" have provided no other explanation for this dramatic and sudden rise in Autism cases, despite a draconian effort to find one.

They attempted to say it was genetic, but geneticists were quick to respond that genetic disorders do not suddenly increase in such astronomical proportions. [It is impossible to have a genetic pandemic.] They then said it was because of better diagnosis, despite the fact that the diagnosis is obvious in virtually every case and that the criteria officially accepted for diagnosis has become **more** restrictive, not less.

When trapped by a lack of evidence, defenders of a nefarious position resort to their old standby—the epidemiological study.

Statisticians will tell you that the least reliable type of study is an epidemiological study because it is so easy to manipulate the data so that the study tells you anything you wish it to. Every defense offered by vaccine defenders is based on such studies, and never the actual science. Then they announce that the issue is settled and no further studies need to be done. After the media has been informed that the issue has been settled, those who continue to present the evidence are considered kooks . . . and ignorant. [i.e. "Conspiracy Theorists."]

The globalist's intend childhood vaccinations to be used as a tool for depopulation and for creating a cognitive deficit among the global citizenry. Dr. Tenpenny has this to report:

The whole cell pertussis vaccine, first introduced in 1923, often caused profoundly adverse effects on a child's developing brain, resulting in permanent changes in behavior, personality, intelligence, emotional stability, and physical ability. In the 1985, A Shot in the Dark, a book by Barbara Loe Fisher and Harris Coulter, PhD, estimated that 1,000 babies died every year from the whole cell pertussis vaccine and more than 12,000 suffered from permanently damaged brains. When these numbers were presented to Congress, the information was compelling enough to lead to the passage of the National Childhood Vaccine Injury Act of 1986. The upside of this legislation is that it gives parents and individuals a path to file for compensation from the government for injuries caused by a vaccine without the gristmill of a lawsuit. The downside is that because the law shields vaccine manufacturers from all product liability and litigation, they have no incentive to create safer, less toxic products. Therefore, neither the government (CDC/FDA/NIH) nor the pharmaceutical industry has any reason to evaluate their products—vaccines—for synergistic toxicities.

Throughout the 1940s into the 1960s, physicians insisted on vaccinating with whole cell pertussis vaccines—even though they knew it was causing brain damage—claiming, "It is the only vaccine we have to prevent pertussis." During that time vaccine manufacturers hid the fact that whole-cell pertussis vaccines contained high levels of pertussis endotoxin, the primary cause of brain inflammation.

In 1943, Dr. Leo Kanner's seminal paper described 11 cases of a form of mental illness never seen before in children. This condition soon became known as autism. It may not be a coincidence that autism—and Asperger's syndrome—appeared around the same time as the whole cell pertussis vaccine became widely used.

Beginning in the early 1960s, and virtually every year until the mid-1980s, at least one research paper was published annually on the association between irreversible brain injury and the whole cell pertussis vaccine. It is a human travesty that the acellular pertussis vaccines—which have less pertussis toxin—was not accepted for widespread use in the US until 1997, more than 75 years after this safer vaccine was first manufactured. Acellular pertussis vaccines are now used exclusively in the US, but the neurotoxic whole cell pertussis vaccines are still used worldwide. For example, between 2005 and 2015, more than 110 million doses of whole cell pertussis vaccines were distributed around the world annually through UNICEF.

The Corona Virus vaccine is an influenza-type vaccine, yet such vaccines do not protect against influenza-like illnesses caused by other types of pathogens. (There are over 200 different types of Influenza pathogens. Corona Virus is only one species of Influenza, and is listed in the Medical Encyclopedia, Medline Plus, as the causal agent for the *Common Cold.*) All these pathogens manifest the same symptomologies: fever, headache, aches and pains, cough and nasal congestion. Influenza and influenza-like illnesses are of brief duration and typically do not result in death or physical complications. (Except for immuno-compromised elderly. Statistics show the highest death rate from upper respiratory diseases is among the over 65 demographic. Their deaths are unrelated to any fake pandemic.)

The evidence presented throughout this volume proves that the Covid vaccine and all previous bioweaponized vaccines, and those to come, are specifically formulated to induce disease, weaken or inactivate naturally-conferred immunity, cause sterility and premature death. (Death is not caused by the alleged virus, but is the result of the virus-replicating vaccine.) It is the vaccine itself which is the principal means utilized by the globalists to debilitate and depopulate.

VACCINE TOXICITY:
DELIBERATELY DAMAGED CHILDREN

The financial cost of vaccine injury is nominal compared to the irreparable damage done to the vaccinated child. Studies indicate that 54 percent of American children have one or more vaccine-induced chronic diseases. The actual percentage figure is actually much higher because many of the families cannot afford the care and testing necessary to properly diagnose the child's vaccine-acquired disability. Subsequent to the passage of the National Childhood Vaccine Injury Act of 1986 and the creation of the National Vaccine Injury Compensation Program (a federal no-fault mechanism for compensating vaccine-related injuries or deaths by establishing a claim procedure involving the United States Court of Federal Claims), vaccine companies, the medical community, and insurance companies were enabled to operate without legal oversight and accountability for vaccine injury. The Public Readiness and Emergency Preparedness Act (PREPA or the PREP Act) became law in 2005, adding to corporate freedoms from liability. According to Wikipedia, this Act "is a controversial tort liability shield intended to protect vaccine manufacturers from financial risk in the event of a declared public health emergency. The act specifically affords to drug makers immunity from potential financial liability for clinical trials of . . . vaccines at the discretion of the Executive branch of government. PREPA strengthens and consolidates the oversight of litigation against pharmaceutical companies under the purview of the secretary of Health and Human Services." Pharmaceutical and biotech companies are free from vaccine injury litigation by calling their *weaponized biowarfare concoctions* "vaccines." This enables them to generate massive profits without incurring liabilities. Immune from litigation, government regulations and laws, these criminal organizations can create a guaranteed market through legislative mandates.

Pharmaceutical companies, such as Pfizer and Moderna, have been given the administrative role of the FDA's regulatory authority. This represents a conflict of interest and is indicative of the protocol to vaccinate without government approval, thus enabling the globalists to achieve their depopulation agenda unhindered.

FAKE PANDEMIC VACCINES ARE NOT MEDICINE

The term, "Vaccine," is deceptively being used as a misnomer to mask the reality which the globalist's do not want the rest of the world to realize. The Covid injected vaccine concoction is not designed as a pathogenic preventative, but rather is designed to *create disease*, alter the human genome, and gain access to restructure the human brain. The truth about the new generation of vaccines is that they are *nanotechnology bioweapons*, not medicine.

In addition to bioengineered viruses and pathogenic bacterial strains, toxic heavy metals—including Mercury, Aluminum, Lead and Arsenic—are present in all vaccines. While they toxify every cell in the body and disrupt the chemical and electrical processes of the central nervous system, these lethal chemical elements reduce an individual's energy level and adversely affect cognitive functions such as memory, problem solving, and processing complex information. The gene-splicing capability of the new generation of fake pandemic vaccines such as Covid, shut down the immune system and foster a dependency upon further biowarfare vaccines; they confer no immunity, but rather genetically code for the disease. Bioengineered viral/bacterial components in vaccines produce delayed-onset stealth diseases such as Cancer and Diabetes later in life. This information is censored by the Illuminati-controlled media, and no doctor, except for a rare few, are either aware of vaccine bioweaponry or are willing to make it known. Nongovernment-funded research proving the dangers of vaccines and their link to disease and mortality is blacklisted, discredited, suppressed from peer review and denied access by the public.

In 2017, Italian researchers reviewed the ingredients of 44 types of so-called "vaccines" and discovered heavy metal debris and biological contamination in every vaccine they tested. The researchers stated, "The quantity of foreign bodies detected and, in some cases, their unusual chemical compositions baffled us." Their conclusion was that, since the contaminants were "neither biocompatible nor biodegradable," they could cause inflammatory and other adverse affects. The consistent toxic composition was a deliberate and intentional component of the vaccine concoction and was "biopersistent" with the effect that it could present immediately or manifest as *delayed-onset symptomologies* at some future time. Aborted fetal tissue and animal tissue was also found to be present. [Gatti AM, Montanari S (2016) New Quality Control Investigations on Vaccines: Micro and Nanocontamination. Int J Vaccines Vaccin 4(1): 00072. DOI: 10.15406/ijvv.2017.04.00072].

The vaccines of the past are mild by comparison to those being bioengineered in today's gene-splicing biotechnology laboratories. The administration of the vaccine *biowarfare agents* listed above are the new generation of vaccines that not only contain toxic heavy metal ingredients which cause diseases and sterility, but also components of injectable digital nanotechnology to enable surveillance, a financial system of debits and credits, gene-splicing, and a mind-link of the human brain to 5G Starlink global WiFi. The nanotechnological components present in the Covid vaccine consists of programmable microchips for digital identity and tracking, and can be remotely turned on and off to exercise ultimate control over the recipient (life and death is literally in the hands of the vaccine-deranged globalists). Clearly, this is not medicine, but is heavy metal poisoning, global surveillance trace and tracking, and nano-robotic brain interface with quantum machines. By calling a *biowarfare agent* a "Vaccine," pharmaceutical, technology, and insurance interests eliminate risk of liability, and the complicit FDA can shield them from scrutiny and transparency by the public.

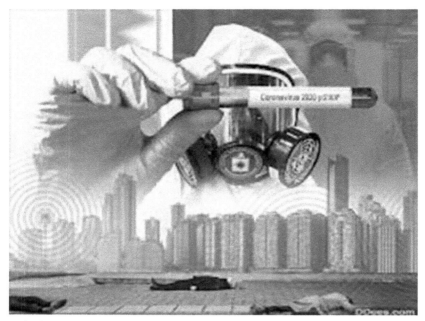

Today's fake pandemic "vaccines" are not medicine; they are a biowarfare assault upon the world population by globalist perpetrators who are protected from financial and legal responsibility.

HOW THEY PLAN TO KILL YOU

The Covid vaccine, and all fake pandemic vaccines to come in the future, are likely to be the first phase of a two-part Binary System (military bioweapon) that can be triggered with a second vaccine or by some other means of activating the death response in humans (5G). This would serve the purpose of the globalist's timing the eradication of large numbers of people to coincide with unrelated events which are not traceable to the adminstration of a vaccine. It also has the advantage of geographically targeting populations for selective elimination. By the ruse of viral "Variants" they will justify the administration of a second, third, or more vaccines.

As a binary weapon having nothing to do with conferring immunity, the administration of a C–19 vaccine represents the first stage of *priming* the immune system to allow for a complete takeover and shutdown of bodily defense systems. The Covid vaccine contains a genetic code for replicating Corona Virus (the entire virus, not just the Spike protein) or any viral species the globalist's may wish to utilize for causing a global death scenario. This nucleotide sequence of three A-T/G-C amino acids (Codon) will code for creating *the virus* once it is present in the body; the bioengineered vaccine tricks the immune system into not attacking the invading organism, but instead replicates it.

Upon the Covid vaccine messenger RNA entering through the selectively permeable cell membrane (there are trillions of cells comprising the human body), and into the cell nucleous, it will make a copy of itself using the cell's own DNA as a template. Then, ribosomal RNA manufactures the proteins to replicate the Corona Virus (or a Variant viral species). Upon exiting out of the cell cytoplasm into the interstitial medium of the body, messenger RNA will encounter the second dose of C–19 vaccine containing the Corona Virus (or other "triggers") and, because the DNA it contains has been altered to not recognize the foreign invader as an enemy and destroy it, the mRNA instead creates a copy of *the virus*. Since the injected mRNA has been genetically engineered to by-pass the body's normal immune response to an invading organism, it is not programmed to destroy the virus, *but will DNA-code for the invading organism.* The totality of human cells will then replicate that pathogen trillions of times over, such that the body is overwhelmed with infection and dies of sepsis, cardiac arrest, or some other organ failure.

The deception is that, once people are vaccinated with the first round of Covid m-RNA, most of them will not manifest a physical reaction, but some will experience illness and may die from anaphalatic shock syndrome or other response to vaccine trauma. (The elderly can, and often do, die from mild forms of the seasonal Flu, with or without having been vaccinated. A bioweaponized "Flu Shot" merely expedites the death process.) Thus, since most will survive the first round of bioweapon injectables, the public will have confidence in receiving future vaccines (Variants), and people's reluctance to be vaccinated will be diminished. But that is the coup which the global madmen are hoping for—a spontaneous rise in the death toll as hundreds of millions die from a second (or third, and subsequent) round of vaccines, perfectly timed so that no one suspects it was actually the *vaccine* that killed them. (They will be told that the cause of death was the Variant virus.) Vaccines permanently shut down the normal immune response so that an individual no longer has natural immunity against disease pathogens, and is thereafter totally dependent upon receiving further injections of bioweaponized death shots.

The media will report deaths as having been caused by Corona Virus, or by a never-ending series of nonexistent *Variant* species of Corona Virus, and thus set up a scenario for more vaccines containing newly bioweaponized genetic sequences that will kill off all those for whom the first round of vaccines were not successful in eradicating. This scenario will perpetuate until the globalist's 95 percent kill rate has been achieved, and the only remaining humans on the planet are those who were not physiologically affected by the fake pandemic weaponized vaccines (5 percent).

THE COVID-19 VACCINE MECHANISM FOR DEATH

Internet Article: **Dr. Lee Merritt: In Animal Studies, After Being Injected With mRNA Technology, All Animals Died Upon Reinfection**

January 29, 2021

In the following interview, Dr. Lee Merritt explains that **mRNA technology is not a vaccine**, mirroring what Dr. David Martin also stated recently.

In animal studies, after mRNA injections have been administered to cats, when the virus arrived once again into the body [exited through the cell membrane to circulate in the systemic blood], it arrived like a Trojan Horse, undetected by the cats' own immune system. The virus multiplied unchallenged and all animals involved in the experiment died from various causes.

According to Dr. Lee Merritt, What happened is all animals died . . . but they didn't die of the "vaccine". What they died from is what used to be called "immune enhancement" and now they call it "antibody dependent enhancement" (ADE).

Here's what happens:

You get the "vaccine" and you do fine. Now, you challenge [inoculate] the animal with the virus that you are supposed to be immunizing against.

So when they challenged those cats with SARS [a.k.a. SARS-CoV-1, is a coronavirus species], instead of killing the virus or weakening it, the immune response that they built into your system went out and coded [replicated] the virus, so the virus came into the cat's body like a Trojan Horse, unseen by the cat's own immune system, and then it replicated without [being recognized and attacked by the body's own immune response] and killed the cat with overwhelming sepsis and cardiac failure. And that [also] happened in ferrets, that happened every time they tried this.

COMMON INFLUENZA RENAMED "COVID"

The present *government-reported* rate of mortality of Covid–19 (at this early stage of global vaccinations) is lower than historical levels of seasonal Influenza (.01% vs .27%) for people under the age of 60. Since this is a very low rate of incidence, why expose yourself to the proven health risk of being injected with a *vaccine* that has been shown by *nongovernment statistics* to have a high probability of disability or death? This argument is especially convincing since the fake pandemic vaccine is not designed to prevent infection, and once you are exposed to the "virus" or other factors coded by the mRNA present in the vaccine, it will trigger the *binary weapon* to produce the virus, which will "go viral." The consequence will be your subsequent untimely death.

A decision to submit to a Covid vaccine represents a fatal error in logic. In consideration of the fact that less than 15 percent of influenza illness each season is caused by influenza viruses, therefore, a vaccine injection is not an effective solution for a cure. (ref. Appendix C for a safe and effective non-vaccine means to cure all illness and disease, including Influenza species such as "Covid.") By calling the "Flu" or Flu-like symptoms, "Covid," and media-promoting it as the cause of a global pandemic, deaths which are being reported due to Covid are not a result of the Corona Virus, but rather are occurring from the C–19 *vaccine* (ref. this Chapter's Section: IS IT "THE FLU" OR "COVID–19"?).

To date, there has been no immunogenicity testing for the Covid vaccine, yet the FDA has approved it for mass distribution. In animal testing, C–19 vaccine injections killed 100 percent of the test group (ref.previous section). In first injection human testing, it caused anaphylactic reactions, a severe immune response that can be life threatening, including difficulty breathing, shock, unconsciousness and death as reactions to the vaccine. Neither Pfizer nor Moderna C–19 vaccines, nor the newest versions such as Johnson & Johnson, AstraZenca and Sputnik V, have been subjected to peer-review scientific scrutiny for ascertaining safety or efficacy. Immunogenicity information is not included in vaccine packaging inserts, and has traditionally been known among the scientific community to confer null validity to a study, especially since the globalist-funded Covid "research" is designed to support their political Agenda, not refute it.

The Covid vaccines contain polyethylene glycol (PEG) which coats the messenger RNA (carrier for the C-19 vaccine) entering bodily cells, and is known to precipitate anaphylactic reactions that trigger anti-drug antibodies (ADA's) which may cause allergic symptoms and death. Bill Gates has estimated that 700,000,000 people will die from the Covid vaccine; other estimates by less conservative globalists are in the billions of deaths worldwide. Presently, after only 6 weeks of the Covid vaccine having become available to select groups (January 1–February 14), vaccine adverse reactions and death rates are increasing exponentially. The Covid vaccine is a *lethal bioweapon* for depopulation and is intended as a means to render recipients cognitively disabled and reduce the world population by 95 percent from the present level of 7.5 billion people. If everyone in the world submitted to the death shot, fewer than half a billion (375 million) human beings would remain alive on the planet after the culling.

A recent February 5, 2021 Article on the Internet is headlined: "45-Year-Old Italian Doctor In the Prime of Life and in Perfect Health Drops Dead After the Pfizer mRNA COVID Shot: 39-Year-Old Nurse, 42-Year-Old Surgical Technician Also Dead" https://humansarefree .com/2021/02/45-year-old-italian-doctor-dead-pfizer-mrna-covid -19-shot.html All three of these deaths were from the same cause— cardiac arrest. Increasingly more sudden deaths are being reported, and the vaccine cause of death is dismissed by the controlled media.

A recent Internet Article: **Pharmacist Gets Vaccinated And Dies. Ausl (Health Authorites): "Vaccine Has Nothing To Do With It"** *By DINO GRENADE Secondopianonews.it*

A 49-year-old pharmacist, Miriam Gabriela Godoy, of Porto Corsini, a seaside resort on the Adriatic coast, died last Wednesday after receiving the anti-Covid vaccine.

This was reported by the Resto del Carlino and Ravenna Notizia that explain how the woman would have died from an illness.

The pharmacist had undergone vaccination on January 14, 2021. The next day she had gone to the pharmacy to work and felt ill. She was urgently transported to the Bufalini Hospital in Cesena, where she died a few days later, Wednesday, January 20th. The woman, who leaves 4 children, had no autopsy performed to ascertain the real causes of death.

Among colleagues—writes the Carlino—someone in recent days has been concerned because the woman had recently received the vaccine when she felt ill: in this regard, Ausl specifies that "there is absolutely no correlation between the vaccine and what happened to the woman."

But really? And how do these "experts" Ausl assert this without carrying out any autopsy, then have in hand evidence that it was not the vaccine [that killed] the woman? A sad story, like so many others, punctuated by many mysteries and omissions. (Source)

49-year-old pharmacist, Miriam Gabriela Godoy, of Porto Corsini, a seaside resort on the Adriatic coast, died last Wednesday after receiving the anti-Covid vaccine.

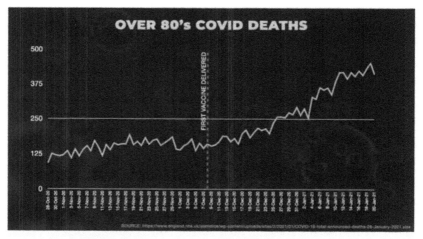

UK Column News - 1st February 2021

The first generation of Covid vaccines are a military-style biowarfare device for deployment against humanity. As a eugenics tool, it targets the elderly.

MARK OF THE BEAST: COVID VACCINE 666
QUANTUM DOT LUCIFERASE TATTOO

Is the Covid vaccine, and all fake pandemic vaccines to follow (Bill Gates has stated there will be 28 of them), the literal Mark of the Beast? If so, does submitting to the *biowarfare injection* void entry into the Kingdom of Heaven? Is it an unredeemable decision which cannot be forgiven by a merciful God? Scripture is very clear that there exists a war against the Saints (Daniel 7:21), and it speaks of a device that sounds exactly like the Corona Virus vaccine biometric quantum dot tattoo Validation Certificate (Revelation 13:16,17). It is known that the Certificate will be embedded into the body, either the right hand or forehead. (It may at first be in the fingerprint side of the index finger.) It is also known that the vaccine will replicate the viral pathogen, change human genetics, and link the recipient to an AI global Neuralink. What is even more compelling is that no one can buy or sell without it. That aspect alone should be sufficient to convince a rational person that the C–19 vaccine is the prophesied *Mark of the Beast.* The diabolical character of vaccines in general, and fake pandemic vaccines in particular, is clear evidence that vaccines are high level witchcraft, Black Magic, Satanism. (Pharmacy/Pharmaceuticals = Pharmakeia (Greek) = Sorcery = Covid Vaccines.)

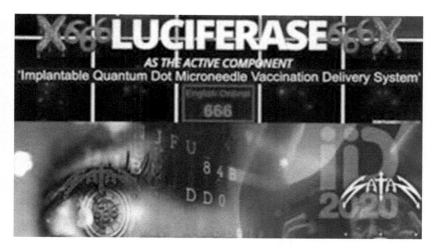

In the last Book of the Bible, Revelation, specifically Chapter 13 verses 16,17, there is foretold of a government-issued "Mark" that is by totalitarian decree and which everyone on the planet must submit to receiving in their right hand or forehead. This 2000 year old prophesy of mandatory compliance to an injected device has today come to pass in the form of a vaccine requiring dermally-embedded digital proof of vaccination.

There will be subsequent versions of the basic vaccine engineering design, and the incremental progression of moving from an injected C–19 vaccine digital ID to the Revelation 13:16,17 Mark of the Beast will be in the form of seemingly innocuous steps toward a high-lighted Luciferase tattoo (bioluminescent ingredient from fireflies) that glows upon the wave of a scanner across the back of the hand or forehead. However, the present early stage of the Covid vaccine also qualifies for Mark of the Beast (i.e. Beast = government) status since it will soon become mandatory, and with the added requirement of a visible form of vaccination proof, which, upon scanning, confirms that an individual has been vaccinated. Without government-approved vaccine validation it will not be possible to buy or sell in any private or commercial sense. This is the key criteria for qualifying as the Revelation 13:17 Mark.

Bill Gates owns the patent for manufacturing the Covid Vaccine and all related patents. The vaccine patent number: WO060606A1 is clearly a designation for the prophesied 666 Mark of the Beast. The implications of the vaccine are, therefore, of an eternal nature and involve not merely the loss of one's personal freedom and life, but also the loss of one's soul.

FUN VAX

Neuroscience has mapped the human brain to identify areas of the neural cortex that are associated with physical sensations and cognitive processes. Some scientists believe they have located an area of the Cerebrum with receptor sites for religious sentiments. Consequently, the globalist mindset has determined to create a vaccine that will inhibit the "impulse" to worship God. They call the vaccine

"ELIMINATE THE SOUL WITH MEDICINE"

theorgonizedearth More than a hundred years ago, Rudolf Steiner wrote the following:

"In the future, we will eliminate the soul with medicine. Under the pretext of a 'healthy point of view', there will be a vaccine by which the human body will be treated as soon as possible directly at birth, so that the human being cannot develop the thought of the existence of soul and Spirit.

To materialistic doctors, will be entrusted the task of removing the soul of humanity. As today, people are vaccinated against this disease or that disease, so in the future, children will be vaccinated with a substance that can be produced precisely in such a way that people, thanks to this vaccination, will be immune to being subjected to the "madness" of spiritual life.

He would be extremely smart, but he would not develop a conscience, and that is the true goal of some materialistic circles.

With such a vaccine, you can easily make the etheric body loose in the physical body.

Once the etheric body is detached, the relationship between the universe and the etheric body would become extremely unstable, and man would become an automaton, for the physical body of man must be polished on this Earth by spiritual will.

So, the vaccine becomes a kind of arymanique force; man can no longer get rid of a given materialistic feeling. He becomes materialistic of constitution and can no longer rise to the spiritual."

-Rudolf Steiner (1861-1925)

"Fun Vax," a pejorative euphemism for *Fun*damentalist Christianity Vaccine that will purportedly eradicate "religious fanatics." This is not a new idea, but was proposed over 100 years ago by an atheist/eugenicist, Rudolf Steiner.

The greatest impediment to a total takeover of America and the world are the people who retain the God of Christianity as their only authority. Those who acknowledge Jesus Christ as the Ruler in all the affairs of men are in diametric opposition to the established order that has usurped the throne and sovereignty of God and masquerades as legitimate figureheads over all the people of the world. These are the unjust, the *basest of men*, who presume a form of righteousness that is an expression of tyranny and brutal injustice. Daniel 4:17: *This matter is by the decree of the watchers, and the demand by the word*

of the holy ones: to the intent that the living may know that the most
High ruleth in the kingdom of men, and giveth it to whomsoever he will,
and setteth up over it the basest of men. In totality, they constitute a
body of like-minded individuals, groups, and institutions which outwardly appear righteous, yet are engaged in usurpation of freedom
and denial of human rights which are the God-ordained liberties for
everyone. They are the progeny of a lesser god, the Servants of the
Lie; they are The Criminal Fraternity. Oppressive rule is their chief
characteristic; human civil government is their religion; Lucifer/
Satan is their god (ref. *The Criminal Fraternity*).

Christian pastors are advising their congregations to take the
Covid vaccine and not be concerned that it is the Biblical Mark of
the Beast. In disobedience to God and in obedience to their government master, Satan, they are in compliance with the CIA's Clergy
Response Team that recruited more than 200,000 Christian leaders
into their globalist indoctrinations. Pastors agreed to tell their trusting congregation to wear masks, maintain social distancing, suspend
Church services, and get vaccinated. They even wear masks while
attending chuch services, transgressing the command of God: *The*
just shall live by faith (Hebrews 10:38). They advise their following
not to worry about vaccine "side effects," which they are told to say,
"will go away within a couple of weeks." For their agreement with
Satan's religion of human government and for their cowardice, pastors all across America will be present in the Lake of Fire. Jeremiah
48:10: *Cursed be he that doeth the work of the LORD deceitfully, and*
cursed be he that keepeth back his sword from blood. For misleading
the ignorant, and for their lies and deceits, many pastors will suffer
the judgment wrath of an angry God: *Because with lies ye have made*
the heart of the righteous sad, whom I have not made sad; and strength-
ened the hands of the wicked, that he should not return from his wicked
way, by promising him life (Exekiel 13:22). Few religious leaders of
today who call themselves "Pastor" are representative of true Biblical
Christianity. Many of them are of the *Synagogue of Satan* (Revelation
2:9, 3:9). This severely damages the image of True Christianity for
those who sincerely wish to know the meaning of their life in a larger

context than their everyday experience. For the hypocritical example which pastors and those calling themselves "Christian" project to the world, they will be judged by God according to their deeds.

Submitting to a *Covid bioweapon* vacccine is like playing with fire, literally. The consequences of receiving the *Covid vaccine biochip* are that it alters chromosomal gene sequencing to change human DNA into nonhuman DNA, and in the process the bearer loses their species identity as a 100 percent human being. Upon 5G Neuralink interface, they consequently forfeit their Will to freely choose. Thus, they are no longer a Free Will agent made in the image and likeness of God. The loss of their volition defaults to the issuer, which is ultimately Lucifer/Satan. It is for this reason that God sternly condemns anyone who submits to the damning *microchip Mark* vaccine, for once a person is "Marked" they cannot reverse the spiritual/genetic damage that has been done, and they are thereby prohibited from entering the Kingdom of Heaven. God gives them over to defilement by the New World Order Luciferians, and hell is their assured destiny.

The Judgment wrath of God is both swift and severe as plagues afflict those many who shall say "yes" to the *Devil's government vaccine*, and who say "no" to the King of kings and Lord of lords, Jesus Christ (Revelation 19:16). While alive on earth they will suffer the punishment of vaccine-induced physical ailments, incurable diseases, plagues and afflictions; and upon death they shall be translated into a place of torment in the center of the Earth. Then, after the return of Jesus, their soul body shall be cast into the outer darkness of a trans-dimensional realm known as the Lake of Fire. There, they will remain for all of eternity because of their unrepentant unrighteousness and because they obeyed Satan's government enablers (doctors, nurses, and other healthcare workers) to receive his Mark via a hypodermic vaccine injection. Consequently, they will be tortured by searing heat, fire, and sadistic demons without cessation. Revelation 14:9-11: *And the smoke of their torment ascendeth up for ever and ever: and they have no rest day nor night, who worship the beast and his image, and whosoever receiveth the mark of his name* (v.11).

Vaccine Protesters line the street outside Dodger Stadium to warn the Sheeple not to get vaccinated with the Covid bioweapon. But to no avail, as the spiritually dead and dying eagerly submitted to being injected with a *nanotech biowarfare agent.*

This is God's final Judgment upon the disobedient—those who, because of their unrighteousness, submit to a weaponized COVID, SPARS, or any other vaccine—trusting in corrupt man rather than a perfect God. But those who stand against Satan's government people, rejecting their lies and diabolical vaccines, and while making public the truth of the Covid deception, must be prepared to sacrifice their life for the sake of The Truth. It will be the best decision *the few* will ever make (Matthew 7:14).

Internet Article: *(CNN)* **A few dozen protesters carrying anti-vaccination signs briefly shut down Los Angeles' largest Covid-19 vaccination site over the weekend.**

The Los Angeles Fire Department temporarily closed the entrance to the Dodger Stadium vaccination site Saturday for 55 minutes, Andrea Garcia, a spokeswoman for Mayor Eric Garcetti, told CNN on Monday.

Hundreds of cars were waiting in line for the vaccine as anti-vaccination protesters held up messages outside, CNN affiliate KCAL/KCBS reported.

Video from the affiliate showed one sign that said, "LA Better Dodge The Vaxxx"; another read "Covid=Scam."

Los Angeles Police Department spokesman Officer Drake Madison told CNN that the protesters were "anti-vaxxers." The gathering was peaceful and no arrests were made, he said.

The protesters may have caused the gates to be closed by authorities out of caution, but they didn't stop people from getting vaccinated during that time, Garcia told CNN. No appointments were canceled.

"The city is reviewing vaccine site safety protocol and will be setting up a protest zone in the event of any future protests," Garcia said in an email.

Dodger Stadium is one of the largest vaccination sites in the country. Garcetti touted the site has the capacity to vaccinate 12,000 people each day, he said the night before the site opened.

More than 31.1 million doses of the Covid-19 vaccine have been administered in the US, according to data published Sunday by the Centers for Disease Control and Prevention. Los Angeles

County has administered 790,902 doses of the vaccine, as of January 25, according to its Department of Public Health.

"Everyone we encountered there who had an appointment was accommodated," Los Angeles Fire Department spokesman Brian Humphrey told CNN on Monday.

The vaccination process has been an emotional one, he said. "It's not only a physical toll but an emotional toll on us as well," Humphrey said. "It's a very touching moment for a lot of these people getting vaccinated. Maybe they've lost their parents or something like that you know, and they're sobbing and we're giving them an injection. We do this thousands of times each day."

The vaccine program is a joint effort between the mayor's office and the fire department, Los Angeles Fire Department spokesman David Ortiz said Saturday. Vaccine appointments run from 8 a.m. until 8 p.m. and more appointments will be offered "as soon as we receive another allotment of vaccinations," he said.

The Covid deception is so deeply entrenched into the belief system of the spiritually lost and dying that no amount of truth can convince them that they have been programmed and mind-controlled to believe the outrageous pandemic lie. This is most evident among the healthcare community of doctors, nurses and hospital staff workers. While some "defected" from the AMA/media stranglehold and became outspoken

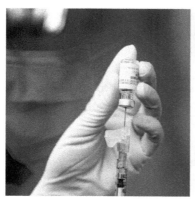 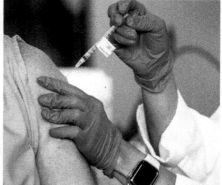

Per the Nuremberg Code, doctors, nurses, and other healthcare workers administering any vaccine, including the C-19 vaccine and all variant vaccines to follow, should be tried as war criminals for crimes against humanity.

whistleblowers exposing vaccines in general, and specifically the pandemic deception and dangers of the Covid bioweapon, they comprise a small minority in comparison to the overwhelming masses of the rabidly deceived "Dr. Mengeles" and "Gestapo nurses" who, under a pretense of public health, daily take up the role of unwitting purveyors of death. Misguided, but sincerely believing in their cause, they never consider that the source of the information upon which they base their criminal actions is the fulfillment of the Globalist's Agenda to depopulate. In the performance of their duties sanctioned by a criminal government, they are the executioners of millions of lives—innocent people who have no idea of the health implications of being vaccinated—and that do not have the option of "informed consent." It was for this reason that doctors were executed during the Nuremberg Trials.

NEW CDC STUDY FINDS MAJORITY OF THOSE INFECTED WITH COVID-19 ALWAYS WORE MASKS

Surgical and cloth masks do not prevent viral transmission. The C-19 pandemic is ostensibly about viral transmission, but face masks have never been shown to prevent or protect against airborne viral contact and have never been recommended for use during the seasonal Flu outbreak, epidemics, or previous pandemics. Therefore, it can be concluded that prevention of the spread of disease is a false rationale for the wearing of masks, and only serves the purpose of a visual means to acknowledge one's submission to the source of the farcical decree. The real reason for the mandated wearing of a mask is not *virus* control, but *people* control. The Luciferian globalists are laughing hysterically at the mass stupidity and ease of deceiving all the world's people (except God's Elect).

The observation is that, to obey an unrighteous illegitimate authority, is to disobey God; and disobedience to God is an indiction that one is not Saved. Believing the Covid lie and submitting to the dictates of a Luciferian criminal government is disobedience to God, and confirms one as a child of a lesser god—Lucifer, Satan the Devil (Hebrews 10:38,39). Therefore, the wearing of a mask, which serves no practical purpose, is a readily visible indicator of submission to

Satan's authority, and indicates a willful and deliberate rejection of God: *Know ye not, that to whom ye yield yourselves servants to obey, his servants ye are to whom ye obey; whether of sin unto death, or of obedience unto righteousness?* (Romans 6:16).

The spiritually dead and dying wear masks which signal their future destiny.

To see this in action, consider today's mass insanity Twilight Zone world and observe all the obedient slaves wearing masks. If they had a working brain they would not wear a mask. A cognitively intact rational person (one with intellectual integrity and a love of the truth) would quickly deduce: "Why wear this? There's no virus, no pandemic, and even if there were, a mask wouldn't help." Mind-controlled pawns watch TV; they believe the propaganda, and therefore they wear a mass. Low IQ people wear masks. Submissive slaves wear masks. Those who will sacrifice the truth in order to make their life easier, wear masks. The ready acceptance of the Covid comic farce demonstrates just how far removed from the reality of God that people truly are; and even more, it shows how many will be in hell. People who willing wear a mask shall also willingly submit to being injected with a soul-destroying 666

Covid vaccine. Therefore, wear a mask, submit to government/submit to Lucifer/Satan, go to hell. It is a logical syllogism.

PEOPLE WHO WILLING WEAR A MASK, OR DEMAND OTHERS TO WEAR A MASK, INDICATE THEIR SUBMISSION AND ALLEGIANCE TO THE GLOBALIST'S AGENDA, AND ARE THEREBY IDENTIFIED AS "UNSAVED"

They:

- Believe the Corona Virus lie

- Are pawns for government control

- Have "Zero" awareness

- Cannot think for themselves

- Shall willingly submit to a *Covid bioweapon* vaccine

- Believe that government tells the truth and cares about them

- Will submit to the soul-damning 666 Mark of the Beast (fake pandemic vaccine)

- By their contempt for those who do not believe the Covid lie and refuse to wear a mask, they confirm that they are not Saved

- Are not as intelligent as those who refuse to wear a mask

- Are blissfully unaware, willfully ignorant and deserve all that is coming

- Obey and serve a Luciferian government—i.e. deny Jesus Christ (Matthew 6:24)

True servants of God do not wear a mask; they obey God rather than men. Acts 5:27–29: *And when they had brought them, they set them before the council: and the high priest asked them, Saying, Did not we straitly command you that ye should not teach in this name? and, behold, ye have filled Jerusalem with your doctrine, and intend to bring this man's blood upon us. Then Peter and the other apostles answered and said, We ought to obey God rather than men.*

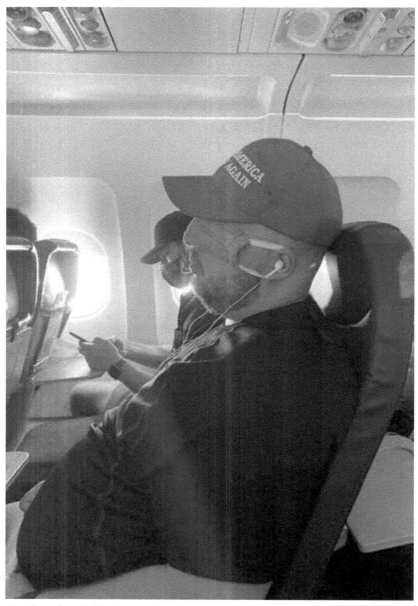

Covid is a laughable farce to a silent minority, but few will stand up and speak out in defense of the truth. Real men do not wear masks; women and castrated neutered males wear masks. The testosterone deficient, pathological compulsive liars, and the deceived uninformed masses insist that others do likewise.

The "Just" trust in God and live by faith. Hebrews 10:38: *Now the just shall live by faith: but if any man draw back, my soul shall have no pleasure in him.* Those who love God keep his Commandments. John 14:15: *If ye love me, keep my commandments.* This explains why virtually everyone you see, wears a mask—they are not just, and they do not love God. If they did love God, they would trust him and live by faith; they would keep his Commandments and obey him; they would refuse to comply with the manipulative lies and deceits of those who presume rulership over them—an illegitimate authority that has usurped the throne and authority of God, and therefore are impostors. A servant of God is under no obligation to recognize or obey impostors.

Obey God and remove the health-endangering mask, which only serves to indicate that your allegiance is with those who perpetuate a lie. Refuse to obey a criminal government run by Satan's government

Submissive slaves believe the Covid lie and wear a mask. The wearing of a mask is an indication of submission to Satan's human government; obeying the lying proclamations of an unjust illegitimate authority = obeying Lucifer/ Satan/the father of lies (Luke 4:5,6; John 8:44).

people. Refuse the *fake pandemic biowarfare* vaccine and do not be among the 2000 people who are cast into the Lake of Fire for every one person who is Saved, and whose destiny is an eternity in Heaven—ref. CH 7 section: SALVATION BY THE NUMBERS (Ecclesiastes 7:28).

WHY I'M NOT WEARING A MASK

With a transmission rate of only 0.2% in an active social arena, wearing masks in a casual environment does not reduce flu infection rates

Article in the California Globe By Michael Robertson, May 5, 2020

San Diego County health officials recently ordered that everyone wear face coverings "anywhere in public when they come within 6 feet of another person" starting May 1, 2020. I do not plan on complying because the scientific research says it does not help and may actually harm people.

Mask wearing is ordered in an earnest attempt to reduce coronavirus infections. It's explained that donning a mask means the infected will spread less virus and the uninfected will be less likely to be infected. Maybe most importantly it will reduce transmission by those who are infected but do not know it because they are at early infection stages or simply never show symptoms as happens with about 50% of those infected. [Author's note: Less than 15 percent of influenza illness or influenza-lke symptoms is caused by influenza virus.]

While this seems logical, the science says it is false. Wearing masks does not reduce influenza infection rate according to an examination of 10 studies looking at this claim. To determine the effectiveness of a procedure requires a randomized controlled test (RCT). Within a population some are given the treatment and others not. By comparing the two populations one can determine if the protocol is effective.

The Center for Disease Control did a pool analysis of 10 RCTs that examined the impact of face masks on reducing influenza infections within a community. They concluded that these studies "found no significant reduction in influenza transmission with the use of face masks." These studies covered a wide range of environmental settings from University dorms to households, but the results were the same across them all.

"There is limited evidence for their [masks] effectiveness in preventing influenza virus transmission," they found. This applied to masks "worn by the infected person for source control OR when worn by uninfected persons." They unambiguously concluded that there was "no significant effect of face masks on transmission of laboratory-confirmed influenza."

Since we know that flu viruses are spread through aspiration, coughing or sneezing, such a result would seem to defy common sense. However it is explainable when examining more closely how the flu spreads. It is spread through continuous extended close contact, and not casual connections.

Research by the National Center for Immunization Research and Surveillance in Australia shows that transmission in COVID–19 infected people, even in close contact with others in a high intensity school environment, is tiny. They arrived at this conclusion by identifying 18 COVID–19 infected individuals and tracing their movements from March to Mid-April 2020. Nine infected students and 9 infected staff across 15 schools were followed. Collectively they had 862 close contacts over this time period. A "close contact" was defined as face to face contact for 15 minutes or in the same room for a minimum of two hours with an infected person. Those in close contact were tested via swabs or blood tests. Of the 735 students and 128 staff members who came in close contact with these 18 cases only 2 infections were identified.

With a transmission rate of only 0.2% in an active social arena such as a school without masks, it's easy to see how wearing masks in a casual environment would not reduce flu infection rates. Specifically since the likelihood of infection from a brief interaction such as a store is so small masks are irrelevant.

It's reasonable to ask if there's possible harm from mask usage. Anyone who has worn one while painting or construction or any extended period of time knows they quickly become moist and slimy, which is the ideal breeding ground for bacteria and viruses. Pathogens trapped in the mask have ideal conditions to grow exposing the wearer to an increased risk unless the mask is disposed of after every use or chemically disinfected. One study looked at 1607 medical care workers and found that cloth masks lead to higher respiratory infection rates. "The rate of influenza-like illness is statistically significantly higher" with cloth masks they concluded. Disturbingly, COVID–19 is an influenza-like virus which attacks the respiratory system, so it's possible cloth mask wearers may have a higher rate of contracting COVID–19. They speculate that, "Moisture retention, reuse of cloth masks and poor filtration may result in increased risk of infection."

There's much we're learning about this pandemic, but the best science we have shows that mask wearing will not reduce transmission because casual contact is not a common source of transmission. Furthermore the cloth masks that many are resorting to may actually increase the likelihood of an infection achieving the exact opposite of the intended result. I call on health officials to look more closely at the science and withdraw their order for mask wearing because the data says it will do more harm than good to residents.

IS IT "THE FLU" OR "COVID-19"?

Covid mRNA vaccines are a military "Binary Weapon" that causes an "Immune Enhancement" delayed death. Some die shortly after receiving the depopulation vaccine (anaphalactic shock, sepsis, respiratory infection, etc); others die a year or two later after being exposed to the immune response "Activator." Part 1 is the injected vaccine containing mRNA gene-altering protein sequences; Part 2 is the trigger which activates the changed genetic program for the body to self-destruct by not recognizing a disease pathogen and instead replicates it by coding for the pathogen's DNA. The trigger could be a second round of vaccines or something else, such as a

5G electromagnetic signal transmitted to the microchip that was injected with the original vaccine. Therefore, a massive death toll is predictable for the near future, and it will not be directly traceable to the Covid death shot. Accountability for sudden local, regional, or global depopulation will consequently be diverted.

Internet Article: **What Happened to the Flu Season? Epidemiologist Says the Flu Has Been Reclassified as COVID-19**

A few months ago, some infectious disease experts began warning that it would be extremely difficult, as the COVID-19 pandemic lingered into the fall, for frontline healthcare providers to determine if sickness was due to the novel coronavirus or good, old-fashioned influenza. Image source: NewsNation Now

The reason, they said, is that in many respects, flu symptoms could and would mimic COVID-19 symptoms.

But according to one epidemiologist, that problem has been solved by the 'powers that be': **Simply reclassify flu cases as COVID-19 illnesses—that way, "flu cases" will go down this year while Joe Biden's authoritarian Democrats get to continue 'justifying' perpetual lockdowns and theft of our liberty and freedom.**

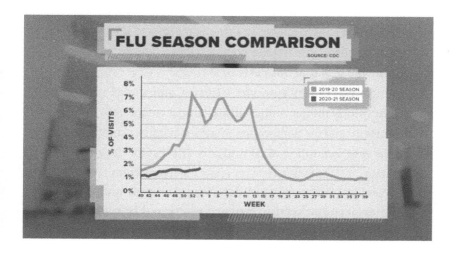

Per Just the News:

Rates of influenza have remained persistently low through late 2020 and into 2021, cratering from levels a year ago and raising the puzzling specter of sharply reduced influenza transmission rates even as positive tests for COVID-19 have shattered numerous records over the last several weeks.

Where have all the flu cases gone?

Epidemiologist Knut Wittkowski thinks he can answer the riddle. **"Influenza has been renamed COVID in large part," Wittkowski, the former head of biostatistics, epidemiology and research design at Rockefeller University, told the outlet.**

"There may be quite a number of influenza cases included in the 'presumed COVID' category of people who have COVID symptoms (which Influenza symptoms can be mistaken for), but are not tested for SARS RNA," he added.

Such patients, he explained, "also may have some SARS RNA sitting in their nose while being infected with Influenza, in which case the influenza would be 'confirmed' to be COVID."

You know, like when you die from a gunshot wound or a car accident but just happen to test positive for the novel coronavirus, it's listed as a COVID death.

But don't just take our word for it or that of Wittkowski; the government's own data shows that something fishy is going on, which has been par for the course when it comes to misrepresenting the threat of this virus.

According to the Centers for Disease Control and Prevention's recent weekly influenza surveillance tracker, cumulative positive flu rates from late September to mid-December only stands at 0.2 percent, according to clinical labs that test for the virus. That compares to last year's very typical 8.7 percent cumulative.

Weekly comparisons of data from last year and this year show an even starker difference: A year ago this week, the positive flu rate was 22 percent, but this year it's just 0.1 percent.

Scientist Has To Hide Identity To Appear On Air And Tell The Truth About COVID-19: Almost No Cases Of Common Flu In Hospitals—All Designated Covid

Some have attempted to explain the humongous difference in flu infections by claiming that mask-wearing, social distancing, and even lockdowns are making the difference.

Timothy Sly, an epidemiology professor at Ryerson University in Toronto, told the outlet that "the reduced incidence of seasonal influenza is almost certainly due to the protection that a large proportion of the population has been using for many months."

Those measures, he said, are "designed to be effective against any airborne respiratory virus."

And Holden Maecker, a professor of microbiology and immunology at Stanford University, agreed.

"I feel pretty confident that the COVID-19 mitigation measures have caused the reduction in flu cases this year," he told Just the News. "Masks, social distancing, and hand washing are all effective counter-measures against colds and flu."

Really? That's just BS; if that were true, then COVID cases wouldn't be spiking at all, anywhere—especially in liberty-free zones like New York and California.

But Maecker had an explanation for that, too. Asked why COVID continues to spread but the highly contagious influenza bug isn't, he said:

"I think it's because (1) there is less pre-existing immunity to SARS-CoV-2 in the population, whereas most of us have had vaccines and/or previous bouts with flu; and (2) the SARS-CoV-2 virus seems to spread more easily than influenza, including more aerosol transmission and 'super-spreader' events. Flu transmission is almost entirely close-range droplets and hand-to-nose or eyes contact."

Again . . . BS. We're being lied to once again about COVID so the authoritarians in our society can continue justifying the elimination of our freedoms.

Academicians and political savants have a vested interest in promulgating Covid lies because their reputation and job are at stake. Therefore, the greatest likihood of falsehoods are from the "Authorities" and "Experts." Even a child is capable of deducing from the data that historical rates of reported influenza have plummeted during the same period that Covid rates are sharply advancing, and therefore, the "Flu" has simply been renamed "Covid."

There categorically is no Covid pandemic, but there does exist a persistent and widespread pandemic of willful ignorance, willingness to believe a lie, and submission to an illegitimate unrighteous authority.

CHAPTER 3

AGENDA 21, AGENDA 2030, ID 2020

"The present vast overpopulation, now far beyond the world carrying capacity, cannot be answered by future reductions in the birth rate due to contraception, sterialization and abortion, but must be met in the present by the reduction of numbers presently existing. This must be done by whatever means necessary."
—A Statement made at the United Nations General Assembly

While surrounded by high-level officials of the FDA and CDC, President Trump announced to a dazed and confused America his plans for combating the Pandemic: "Three hundred and fifty million doses of the Corona Virus vaccine will be distributed by the military, door to door . . ." he stated at an outdoor news conference at the White House. Several days later he responded to a question from one of the reporters when replying, "The vaccine will be on a voluntary basis and no one will be required to take it—only if you think you need it." After making that contradictory proclamation, he gazed over to his handlers standing off to the side, and asked, "Is that a correct statement?" One of the Rothschild's Illuminati agents stepped up to the podium, and in an officious tone declared in a long run-on sentence that ". . . government protocols will be followed . . . to insure the public's safety . . . by compliance with fighting the pandemic . . ." In otherwords, the vaccine would be mandatory and no one would be permitted to escape inoculation with Covid *gene-splicing biowarfare nanotechnology*. In the span of a brief discourse, the leader of the

most powerful nation on earth was countermanded by a representative of the Shadow Government hierarchy, and in so doing proved
that the office of the Presidency is merely a figurehead representation
of an all-encompassing global supra-government acting behind the
cover of an enabling controlled media. Although, while Trump was
President, he appeared to sincerely represent America's interests, he
was working within a framework of pure evil that would not allow
him to make judgments that he was otherwise capable of performing
(ref. Appendix D).

THE AGENDA OF THE GLOBALISTS

America is being destroyed by design, from within, by Federal and
State legislative decrees; and externally, by international govern-
ing organizations such as the United Nations; and by generational
crime families, such as the Rothschilds and Rockefellers. Under the
direction of global Luciferianism the Globalist's Agenda calls for the
creation of sub-agendas that all work toward achieving their End
Game Plan. An Agenda 21 position statement is typical of the Plan:
"By defining and clarifying goals, progress is monitored and assessed
for guiding the overall Agenda to its eventual completion." Specific
goals and dates have been established for when that Agenda (i.e. the
Globalist's Agenda) will be achieved.

One of the primary objectives of the Luciferian global controllers
is to prepare all the world's nation-states for unification under the
purview of a single "supra-government" run by a planetary-wide
leader. It will be a united "One-World" microchipped population
controlled by diabolical dictatorial rule. Agenda 21 and Agenda 2030
are action plans to facilitate that eventual outcome. Drafted by the
UN and signed by 178 governments around the world, among the
stated goals of these documents is the depopulation of humanity
because "we are too many." The Globalist's depopulation Agenda is
promoted by the elites as a means to "Save the Planet."

The United Nations was a forerunner of the supra-government
that presently rules the world from behind the controlled staged

theatrical performance known as "The Media." More properly identified by insiders as "The Illuminati Supreme World Council," the
supra-government (Shadow Government) controls the leaders of all
countries, determines the outcome of Presidential elections, and is
the international entity responsible for enabling a world leader who
shall hold the office of Global President, the biblically prophesied
Antichrist. Anyone who opposes their invisible power or fails to obey
is assassinated, impeached, or shamed out of office. (Lincoln, Kennedy, Nixon, Trump.)

One of the primary functions of the UN/Illuminati Supreme
World Council is not their stated goal of "world peace," but rather
to form and regulate a world standing army, which they refer to as
"Peace-keepers." (Satan's Freemasonry religion always uses the exact
opposite terminology to conceal and obscure word meaning.) A UN
standing army will enforce global laws that supercede any Federal
jurisdictions. By assuming control over any nation's military, that
nation becomes dependent upon the UN, and their military strength
is thereby weakened. Nations are thereby less able to resist when the
Supreme World Council decides to takeover the military role in their
country.

Everything that is occurring today in regard to the Covid fake
pandemic is a direct result of orders sent from the Illuminati World
Council to the hierarchy of the Satanic Pyramid of Power (ref. The
Globalist's Agenda).

OVERVIEW OF THE "PLAN"

The globalists intend to use the ruse of a fake pandemic until their
people control depopulation Agenda is fulfilled. World society will
never return back to the way it was before the start of the Covid
comic farce. It will never get better, and will never revert to normal.

The following is a view of the future from an individual who
occuppied the Federal government position of United States Assis-
tant Secretary of Housing and Urban Development during the Presidency of George H. W. Bush:

"The first and most important goal is the replacement of the existing U.S. dollar currency system used by the general population with a digital transaction system that can be combined with digital identification and tracking. The goal is to end currencies as we know them and replace them with an embedded credit card system that can be integrated with various forms of control, potentially including mind control . . . bankrupting of millions of small and medium-sized businesses. The managers of the dollar system are under urgent pressure to use new technology to centralize economic flows and preserve their control of the financial system. The technocracy that they're pushing towards us is what is called transhumanism. So essentially what you do is you use injections to inject materials into the body that create the equivalent of an operating system. Everybody knows the idea of Microsoft causing you to download an operating system in your computer. That gives Microsoft and a variety of other players a back door into your computer. And every month or two or three you've got to update it because there are viruses, right? It's back to the Magic Virus that can solve all problems. And so this is a similar system for your body. You inject materials into your body that essentially create the equivalent of an operating system and a receiver, and you can literally hook everybody up to the Cloud [Hive Mind]. And that includes hooking them up in a way that their transaction system, you know, the Bible calls it the Mark of the Beast—is one way people know this stuff—but you're basically talking about being able to digitally identify and track people in connection with their financial transactions. So it's a world of zero privacy . . . you then institute one or more central bank cryptos, you're now talking about a system where every central bank in the world can shut you off individually from transacting if they don't like the way you're behaving.

Many people are familiar with the social credit system in China, it's very similar. If you install the smart grid in their car, their community, and now literally in their body, you've got 24/7 surveillance. And if people don't do what you say and behave the way you want, they can and will shut off your money.

And they'll also have spatial control. If they say you can't travel more than five miles, that's it, because you're in a complete digital control system, and it's controlled by the central bankers through the money. We're digitizing everything but it includes the human body as well and the human mind. So this system comes with complete control, not only of your ability to transact financially which is hooked up to your body but very sophisticated mind control technology through the media and those cloud connections. So basically you're talking about hooking up into the "borg" (contraction for cybernetic organism) if you will. And so transhumanism and technocracy go hand in hand.

We have the tech people building the clouds and the telecommunications, we have the military doing space and operation warp speed. So they're putting up the satellites, okay, then we have big pharma which is making the injections that are full of these mystery ingredients and change and modify your DNA, and for all we know to make you infertile. And then we have the media pouring out the propaganda. And then we have the central bankers engineering the crypto, the central bank cryptosystems. So you have these different pillars and it's very important when you look at what's going on day to day, particularly in the media. They're trying to keep them separate so that you can't see how they're going to come together in an integrated system which is basically integrated into your body and your mind.

To institute the slavery system. So in other words, if I am going to do everything through a smart grid and I need to run the smart grid into your neighborhood, and then I need to run the smart grid into your body, the question is how am I going to build it out in your neighborhood and build it on your body without you seeing the trap, right? So that's why you try and keep these different lines separate.

So if you listen to the central bankers, they try as hard as they can to stay away from these conversations. So it was interesting, I was watching an IMF presentation on cross-border payments, and the Federal Reserve chairman, the head of the IMF mentioned the digital global ID system. And the Federal Reserve chairman almost blanched! You could energetically feel him moving like a galaxy away like, "no no no no"! Because [there are] 325 million Americans, and [there are] more than 325 million guns, and he doesn't want everybody to see this until the trap is thrown and it's too late.

Over time, this has evolved to the engineering of epidemics—the medical version of false flags. In theory, these can be "psyops" or events engineered with chemical warfare, biowarfare, or wireless technology.

A SAMPLING OF SUB-AGENDAS OF THE GLOBALIST'S AGENDA

- IS THERE A POWER, A FORCE OR A GROUP OF MEN ORGANIZING AND REDIRECTING CHANGE?

- "EVERYTHING IS IN PLACE AND NOBODY CAN STOP US NOW . . ."

- "PEOPLE WILL HAVE TO GET USED TO CHANGE . . ."

- THE REAL AND THE STATED GOALS

- POPULATION CONTROL

- PERMISSION TO HAVE BABIES

- REDIRECTING THE PURPOSE OF SEX—SEX WITHOUT REPRODUCTION AND REPRODUCTION WITHOUT SEX

- CONTRACEPTION UNIVERSALLY AVAILABLE TO ALL

- SEX EDUCATION AS A TOOL OF WORLD GOVERNMENT

- TAX FUNDED ABORTION AS POPULATION CONTROL

- ENCOURAGING HOMOSEXUALITY . . . ANYTHING GOES HOMOSEXUALITY ALSO WAS TO BE ENCOURAGED.

- TECHNOLOGY

- FAMILIES TO DIMINISH IN IMPORTANCE

- EUTHANASIA AND THE "DEMISE PILL"

- LIMITING ACCESS TO AFFORDABLE MEDICAL CARE MAKES ELIMINATING ELDERLY EASIER

- PLANNING THE CONTROL OVER MEDICINE

- ELIMINATION OF PRIVATE DOCTORS

- NEW DIFFICULT TO DIAGNOSE AND UNTREATABLE DISEASES

- SUPPRESSING CANCER CURES AS A MEANS OF POPULA-TION CONTROL

- INDUCING HEART ATTACKS AS A FORM OF ASSASSINATION

- EDUCATION AS A TOOL FOR ACCELERATING THE ONSET OF PUBERTY AND EVOLUTION

- BLENDING ALL RELIGIONS . . . THE OLD RELIGIONS WILL HAVE TO GO

- CHANGING THE BIBLE THROUGH REVISIONS OF KEY WORDS

- "THE CHURCHES WILL HELP US!"

- RESTRUCTURING EDUCATION AS A TOOL OF INDOCTRINATION

- MORE TIME IN SCHOOLS, BUT THEY "WOULDN'T LEARN ANYTHING."

- CONTROLLING WHO HAS ACCESS TO INFORMATION

- SCHOOLS AS THE HUB OF THE COMMUNITY

- SOME BOOKS WOULD JUST DISAPPEAR FROM THE LIBRARIES . . ."

- CHANGING LAWS

- THE ENCOURAGEMENT OF DRUG ABUSE TO CREATE A JUNGLE ATMOSPHERE

- ALCOHOL ABUSE

- RESTRICTIONS ON TRAVEL
- THE NEED FOR MORE JAILS, AND USING HOSPITALS AS JAILS
- NO MORE SECURITY
- CRIME USED TO MANAGE SOCIETY
- CURTAILMENT OF AMERICAN INDUSTRIAL PRE-EMINENCE
- SHIFTING POPULATIONS AND ECONOMIES—TEARING THE SOCIAL ROOTS
- SPORTS AS A TOOL OF SOCIAL CHANGE
- SEX AND VIOLENCE INCULCATED THROUGH ENTERTAINMENT
- TRAVEL RESTRICTIONS AND IMPLANTED I.D.
- FOOD CONTROL
- WEATHER CONTROL
- KNOW HOW PEOPLE RESPOND—MAKING THEM DO WHAT YOU WANT
- FALSIFIED SCIENTIFIC RESEARCH
- TERRORISM
- FINANCIAL CONTROL
- SURVEILLANCE, IMPLANTS, AND TELEVISIONS THAT WATCH YOU
- HOME OWNERSHIP A THING OF THE PAST
- THE ARRIVAL OF THE TOTALITARIAN GLOBAL SYSTEM

AGENDA 21

As a UN-funded Commission on Global Government, Agenda 21 began meeting in 1992 with the stated premise of worldwide economic development and protection of the environment. Adopting a theme of "Sustainable Development," it was known as the Rio de Janero Earth Summit, and addressed climate change, biodiversity, forestry, and a list of development practices comprising Agenda 21. After four years they published their final report, entitled, "Our Global Neighborhood." Included among its outlined objectives were:

1) Create a centralized worldwide economic/banking currency.

2) Create a world standing army under the direction of the UN Secretary General.

One is given pause to ask, "What does a Socialist system of centralized banking with a global currency, and an international military global standing army have to do with economic development and protection of the environment?"

The 'Earth Summit' also led to the establishment of the Convention on Biological Diversity, and the United Nations Framework Convention on Climate Change (UNFCCC), which was the predecessor of Al Gore's imaginary "Global Warming" and the subsequent need for a "Carbon Tax" to penalize the citizenry for human emmissions of Carbon Dioxide. (Scientific evidence shows that the mean temperature of the Earth has remained constant over the course of hundreds of years. Any "Warming Effect" is not widespread, but local to certain geographic regions, and is the result of the Chemtrail occlusion of the skies (ref. Appendix E) creating a "Greenhouse Effect" that traps infrared radiation from the sun in a lower atmosphere "heat sink" that prevents cooling of the Earth's surface. Gore's false claims are politically motivated to serve the Globalist's Agenda.)

Agenda 21 was defined by its perpetrators as: ". . . a comprehensive plan of action to be taken globally, nationally, and locally, by organizations of the United Nations system, governments, and Major Groups in every area in which humans impact on the environment. . . an action plan for addressing and mobilizing key government agencies and non-government organizations to *control large populations of people* . . ." The "control of people" statement is the key to discern

Agenda 21 true intentions; the real purpose is to herd the great masses of people into "Smart Cities" where they can be monitored by video surveillance, branded with a digital ID (ID2020), and tracked by GPS satellites to forever remain under the watchful eye of the globalist's "Hunger Games" ruling class. A drastic reduction in the human population by weaponized vaccines that sterilize and kill, the electronic 5G WiFi control grid, and perpetual lock down Martial Law will insure a pacified, enslaved and tracked world population that is easy to control.

Whenever the power elites speak, the intention is always to deceive; their words should never be taken literally but must be seen as a "smoke screen" to conceal their true plans and objectives. If the people were ever to discover the actual purpose of the globalist's organized effort, the elites would fail miserably, losing control over the world populous and facing severe opposition from self-aware well-informed individuals and groups that can prevent them from executing their diabolical madness.

AGENDA 2030: THE WILDLANDS PROJECT

The 2030 Agenda for Sustainable Development is a continuation of Agenda 21. It's stated goals are to "eradicate poverty and attain sustainable development worldwide by the year 2030 . . . a shared global vision . . . a plan of action for the people, planet, and prosperity . . . strengthening a larger freedom . . . eliminating poverty in all its dimensions." As a subcategory of the earlier proposed Agenda 21, it furthers New World Order totalitarianism by achieving total people control in the name of environmental salvation. The pretense of a "global vision" consists of 17 Sustainable Development Goals to be achieved by the year 2030, and includes plans for mass microchipping of the world population with Biometric Identification that will be stored in a universally linked supercomputer database in Geneva Switzerland.

In stark contrast to the globalist's cover story, the true objective of Agenda 2030 is the depopulation of humanity, mandatory vaccinations under the pretense of a global pandemic, use of police and military force, Starlink satellite GPS 5G citizen tracking, constant camera surveillance in mega-cities where large concentrations of "global citizens" are subject to a social credit score system (already exists in China) which punishes the citizenry for not complying with hundreds of petty government rules and regulations. Those who refuse to be vaccinated will be fined, jailed, force-vaccinated, and sent to FEMA "Re-education Centers."

According to its documentation, Agenda 2030 is ". . . a comprehensive blueprint for the reorganization of human society." It is backed by Luciferian globalists such as the Rothschilds, Rockefellers, George Soros, Maurice Strong, and Bill Gates, all believing that a large reduction in the world's people is a means to "save the planet." Adopted in 2015, and endorsed by most countries, it has been aggressively promoted and funded by these genocidal multitrillionaires and billionaires who strive for a digital ID microchipped world population surveillanced by a global network of 42,000 low-orbit 5G citizen spy satellites launched by Elon Musk's SpaceX corporation.

On June 13, 2019, The World Economic Forum and the United Nations signed a Strategic Parnership Framework that proposed ". . . outlining areas of cooperation to deepening institutional engagement and jointly accelerate the implementation of the 2030 Agenda for Sustainable Development." While the terminology and proposed goals are intentionally deceptive, the language used in this document speaks of a government/corporate Facist state ruled by globalist entities such as Monsanto, Dupont, Pfizer, and other key Fortune 100 companies. It outlines objectives for a global government takeover of every nation; dismantling national sovereignty and individual property rights, restricting food distribution as a means of people control, and the implementation of other draconian means to deceive, control, and reduce the global population. The outward pretense of humanitarian concerns is always a "red flag" when dealing with psychopathic eugenicists with an Agenda to depopulate.

ID 2020

Digital identity, per the Covid Credentials Initiative, is a fingerprint scan ID Vaccine Certificate. Covid Credentials Digital Identity was first suggested to the National Institute of Allergy and Infectious Diseases (NIAID) by Bill Gates who imagined a scannable digital fingerprint to indicate who has been tested, recovered, or been administered any Corona Virus vaccines. This would insure quarantine compliance and maintain lockdown citizen surveillance to facillitate optimum people control. The use of Smart Phones for time-stamped "selfies" will be a means to provide Online verification of one's vaccine status using mobile phone numbers.

ID 2020 is "An alliance of public and private partners, including UN agencies and civil society." In the globalist's 'Brave New World Order' it requires a Digital ID that will be indelibly tattooed on the back side of the right hand or forehead, and which becomes visible upon luminescent scanning. Without the ID a person will not be able to make buy or sell transactions and will thus be unable to conduct personal business or purchase food, goods, and services. Refusal to submit to the vaccine ID shall result in being denied survival essentials that inevitably result in homelessness and starvation that will likely conclude with arrest and imprisonment.

According to the globalist's propaganda, ID2020 is a nongovernmental organization which "advocates digital ID for the billion undocumented people worldwide." Such disinformation fails to specify the true goals intended by the ID coup of humanity—the real purpose is to trace and track everyone on the planet, mark and locate individuals for determining their specific whereabouts, vaccination status, and their round up and subsequent incarceration or extermination.

ID2020 is a Biometric digital identification that will soon become mandatory for everybody in the world, creating a "globally unified citizenry" where each person is identified by a luciferase (glowing) biometric quantum dot tattoo on the back of their right hand or forehead. Everyone on the planet will be required to receive a (fake pandemic) vaccine that contains genetics-altering gene-splicing nanotech components linking them to the 5G Neuralink/Starlink human control grid. By one's submission to the mandatory vaccine government decree, they swear their allegiance to a worldwide Dictator, also known as the Antichrist. Enslaved within an invisible technetronic cage, it will be a world of forgotten freedom and government tyranny designed to obliterate liberty and the human Will. Most of these protocols are currently in place and are now being implimented; the remainder are in the early stages of operation and scheduled for full deployment in the near future.

Contact Tracing is an aspect of ID 2020 that operates under the pretense of locating and identifying "suspect infected subjects in order to stop the spread of the disease." It is a term originated by the world controllers to describe the tracing and tracking of those people "suspected" of being infected with any of the many fabricated imaginary Covid strains. Contact Tracing involves surveillance to monitor the speed of the viral transmission in order to discern patterns of the disease progression. The globalist's World Health Organization recommends "Active surveillance of populations, with a focus on case finding, testing, and Contact Tracing in all types of demographic scenarios. C–19 surveillance is expected to monitor epidemiological trends, rapidly detect new cases, and based upon this information provide feedback to conduct risk assessment and guide disease preparedness." By means of yet another fraudulent pretense, the Supreme World Council (supra-government Luciferians) will have installed their global dictatorship of total planetary control. They will be able to force vaccine compliance among all the world's people by requiring them to surrender their identity in order to prevent anyone from escaping their *bioweapon* vaccination coup of humanity.

A tracked and traced digitized world populous is in fulfillment of Revelation prophesy. "Monitoring the spread of a nonexistent disease" enables the globalist's to advance closer to their ultimate objective of a microchipped population made possible by the injection of biotechnological gene-splicing tracking *nanotech* vaccines. Continuous monitoring of vaccine recipients and collateral quarantines are essential components of the prophesied Mark of the Beast (Revelation 13:16,17).

While Agenda 21 and Agenda 2030 are merely obfuscation documents for totalitarian rule by the global elites, they strive to make a plausible pretense for preservation of the environment and sustainability of natural resources. Yet, the true objective is always global depopulation and microchipping by means of vaccination. False and misleading statements and ulterior motivation are the standard modus operandi of the Luciferian globalist's who rarely tell the truth. (Whatever is seen or heard on the mainstream News; whatever has its source from the government and the government-controlled media, is 100% guaranteed to be a lie. Flip it over, reverse it, and *that* will be the truth. Everyone in government or the media is a complicit cowardly liar.) Three former Illuminati shill "U.S. Presidents"—Clinton, Bush Jr., Obama—stand before a TV camera and tell the American people to get vaccinated. "Save lives by vaccinating you and your children against a deadly Corona Virus pandemic . . ." they state, a derisive smirk on their lying face. President of the U.S. Foundation, Timothy Wirth, stated in a public address, "We got to ride this global warming issue. Even if the theory of global warming is wrong, we will be doing the right thing in terms of economic and environmental policy." Observe the duplicity of how he links the economy to environmental policy. While the Globalist's Agenda functions under the pretense of environmental issues, public health, and world peace; Malthusian population reduction is always its core objective. Superficial rationale serves a convenient purpose, since the average person has no means to assess or evaluate whether or not there actually exists a problem of overpopulation on the planet. Official UN statements regarding the carrying capacity of the earth are false; the planet is far from exceeding its natural resources, and space to populate is not limited. Deliberate food shortages, sabotaged food distribution, planned reduced agricultural production, and plant genetic modification are globalist strategies to eliminate what they consider to be "excess people." (Food is being denied needy third-world countries and dumped into the ocean or land fills in an effort to sanction or depopulate starving nations such as Africa and China.) The real Agenda is not "overpopulation," but rather *planetary genocide* at the direction of the Luciferian globalists.

The world controllers are not concerned about "global warming," the planet's "carrying capacity," "overpopulation," or any other false flag issues they propose. The only matter of importance to them is the elimination of as many people as possible from the face of the earth, while at the same time exercising total control over human perceptions and Free Will. Working toward their stated goal of the eradication of 95 percent of humanity, all their lesser agendas for promoting a fake pandemic, concern for the environment, media propaganda, etc., are merely a means toward achieving that end. With a remaining world population of 5 percent of present levels after their culling process, the international elites calculate that figure will suffice as the needed infrastructure *to serve them*. As Ted Turner, a Luciferian globalist, has stated: "A total world population of 250–300 million people—a 95 percent decline from present levels—would be ideal." Currently, that number represents the planned genocide of 7.25 billion people.

With the fake pandemic Covid *bioweapon depopulation* vaccine, the Globalist's Agenda End Game is well underway. "The Cull" has begun.

NO WAR ON TERROR

Most people would be shocked, appalled, and offended by any suggestion that there were no terrorists behind the September 11 destruction of the NYC World Trade Towers. That belief is in conflict with programming they received through the media, which indelibly etched upon their mind the many falsehoods required to successfully indoctrinate Americans with a fabrication so preposterous that it should more properly be considered as a comedy skit.

There is no "War on Terror." In order for there to be a war on terror, there must be terrorists. But, except for the Luciferian globalists, there are no terrorists in the sense of a foreign group, individuals, or organizations secretly plotting and executing acts of terror. As insider, Nicholas Rockefeller, heir to the Rockefeller Dynasty and member of the CFR, in regard to 911, reiterated: "There's no real enemy. The War on Terror is a giant hoax. It's a way for the government to take over the American people . . . there's going to be a war on terror [and he's laughing] . . . 911 was done by people in our own government and our own banking system to perpetuate the fear of the American people and to subordinate themselves to anything the government wants them to do, and to create an endless war on terror . . . it's just going to go on and on, so you can never define a winner . . . there are no terrorists . . . the end goal is to get everybody chipped, to control the whole society . . . and if the people don't go along with it and don't do what we want, we just turn off their chip." This statement was made by an individual who possessed detailed information about the Globalist's Agenda (ref. Alex Jones 12/2017 interview with documentary film producer, Aaron Russo: https://www.youtube.com/watch?v=oygBg6ETYIM&list=PL07KE7dr_SSCpMuwyd2ZYpG4XyMc6BSAr&index=6.

The "War on Terror" is actually a war on truth, and against those who tell it. (Aaron Russo was murdered shortly after the airing of the YouTube video.) The Corona Virua fake pandemic is yet another fake war on terror. Like the 911 lie, there is no real enemy, no deadly virus, and the terror is a perpetual never ending series of planned trauma—"Variants," more imaginary viruses to fear, more compulsory vaccines, more oppressive government control. As with 911, the Covid objective is people-control, media disinformation, loss of personal freedom and liberty.

GLOBAL INFECTIOUS DISEASE "FIREFIGHTERS"

Looking ahead to the next planned "pandemic," Bill Gates envisions a "Global Alert System" consisting of 3000 first responders that would rush to the scene of unusual sickness anywhere in the world, where they would perform rapid testing and genetic sequencing.

His "Mega-testing Diagnostic Platforms" could allow screening of more than 100 million people every week, and would consequently serve as an ongoing mechanism to fan the fake news flames of a world consumed by the ravages of an imaginary, but useful, threat. In this manner the global psychopaths would be able to contain any spontaneous "fires" that might flare and precipitate an inconvenient citizen revolt against manufactured tyranny. It is an effective tool for maintaining a lockdown society.

COVAX, an abbreviation for COVID-19 Vaccines Global Access, consists of a data base to "accelerate the development, production, and equitable access to COVID-19 tests, treatments, and vaccines." As a global collaboration among all nations, it is a tool for rapid distribution of vaccines, enabling the sharing of disinformation to instantaneously respond to any fake pandemic which the globalist's may wish to stage. Directed by the World Health Organization and the Coalition for Epidemic Preparedness Innovations, it was created by infamous Bill Gates under the banner of his vaccine awareness

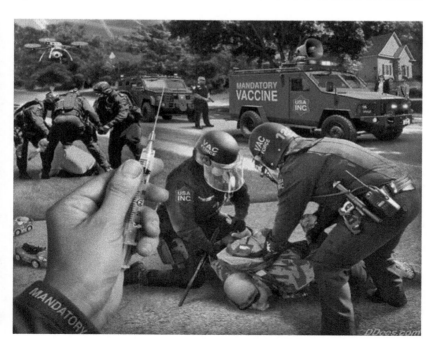

campaign, Global Alliance for Vaccines and Immunization (GAVI), an organization that provides death shot vaccines to the world's poorest people. In anticipation of the soon coming global dictatorial government, this so-called "ACT Accelerator" makes possible a unified world synchronized to function in a globally-centralized political system of international control. First responder mobile vaccine units can be rapidly deployed anywhere in the world, testing, vaccinating and inoculation with gene-splicing, tracking, Luciferase biowarfare agents.

Working with the WHO and contributing to the COVAX Facility, the Gates Foundation has taken measures to insure a readily available supply of vaccine bioweaponry at an affordable price for poor countries. By constantly expanding his worldwide depopulation campaign, Gates' messianic mission to save the world by killing off nearly everyone continues to improve efficiency for increasing the death rate and human body count. (Gates has personally murdered in cold blood over 100 million innocent people in Africa with his vaccines administered under the pretense of public health. In utilizing the fake Covid pandemic bioweapon vaccines he will continue to be the undisputed most prolific serial killer in the history of mankind.)

Regular pandemic simulations, in the manner of Event 201, are in the planning stage for inducing more human-control measures. Predictive programming for germ warfare—Gates calls them "Germ Games"—will be of vital importance for health systems and governments to rapidly gear up for the sudden announcement of yet another act of faked bioterrorism. "Speed matters in a pandemic," said Gates. "The faster you act, the faster you cut off exponential growth of the virus." And also, the faster you eliminate people, which is the underlying purpose of every program launched to stop the spread of the Covid fake pandemic and all future fake pandemics.

REALITY SUMMARY:

1) All acts of "Terrorism" are staged to serve the Globalist's Agenda.

2) Covid vaccines are not a response to any virus, but are an End Game strategy intended by the globalists for depopulation. The biometric quantum dot Luciferase tattoo vaccine Validation Certificate is the Revelation 13:16,17 Mark of the Beast.

3) The following are key dates when individual decisions will be made for heaven or hell; obedience to God, or obedience to satanic government:

   • December 21, 2020: Winter Solstice: First C–19 vaccines available to select groups.

   • June 21, 2021: Summer Solstice: C–19 vaccines available to the public.

   • September 22, 2021: Autumn Equinox: C–19 vaccines mandatory.

4) The wearing of masks (2nd degree of transgression against God), and submission to any of the fake pandemic vaccines (1st degree) are indicators of one's unSaved status. According to Scriptures, 1999 out of every 2000 people (Ecclesiastes 7:28) are judged and condemned to hell. This explains why so many people sheepishly comply with Socialist demands to conform to tyranny, and in so doing, are in disobedience to God.

5) The U.S. and global stock markets are most likely to experience a severe and prolonged decline between the years 2022–2025/2027. (The author forecasted this in 2017.) That period will coincide with Covid fake pandemic Globalist's Agenda End Game scenarios, economic chaos, and social unrest. As a consequence of a worldwide economic crash, a world currency will be the outcome of a devalued U.S. Dollar; all the global currencies will immediately follow.

CHAPTER 4

LIFE UNDER MARTIAL LAW: QUARANTINES, LOCKDOWNS, AND THE "NEW NORMAL"

"Ultimately, a world comprised of isolated and highly fragmented communities with widespread access to information technology— dubbed the Echo Chamber—was selected as the future in which the perspective scenario would take place."
—Scripted planned projection of a future pandemic.
From Johns Hopkins Center for Health Security:
"A Futuristic Scenario for Public Health Risk Communicators"

The 911 fake War on Terror was a proven strategy used by the globalists to create an artificial enemy for diseminating wide spread terror to paralyze the citizenry with fear and gain acceptance of their global control Agenda. Strategic fear is a people-control mechanism which Hitler, Stalin, and other depots throughout history utilized to bring about totaltarian change. The fake Covid pandemic is based upon that same concept—an invisible enemy—to induce fear, trauma, shock, inactivity, and thereby neutralize the potential for an enraged backlash by the people, should they discover the truth about what is being done to them. The manifold aspects of the globalist's plan are hidden from public view and compartmentalized in various corporations and government organizations until the final moments when the sting operation is deployed and takes everyone by surprise. Psychological emotional manipulation and trauma-based mind-control techniques are utilized to condition the public and gain their support before they can figure out what is going on. This is accomplished through the controlled media which repeats an endless loop of fabricated scenarios that override any critical thinking capability among the targeted world population. Falsehoods and deceit are the globalist's primary weaponry for people control.

The Covid "invisible enemy" virus enables maximum government control over people's lives. They can be silenced by fear of punishment, peer pressure, paralyzing media indoctrination, vaccine injections, financial incentives and personal sanctions that neutralize them from organizing and gathering in groups. Citizen spies are everywhere; the self-righteous neighborhood snitch is ubiquitous and only too happy to do his or her "patriotic duty" by reporting "suspicious activity" to the police. Contact Tracing is an excuse for surveillance under the pretense of protection against a nonexistent threat which enables centralization of political power into a global entity that controls every aspect of world society, politics, banking, healthcare, education, and even what people think and believe.

In 2014, computer technology mogul, Bill Gates, was interviewed on a public forum in which he stated that "A pandemic would kill 10 million *excess* people per year." The multi-billionaire's slip of the tongue was heard by millions of Google YouTube viewers before that Internet dominate force responded to their Illuminati masters by deleting the damaging indictment from their public media platform. The former head of Microsoft Corporation played a leading role in utilizing weaponized vaccines to decimate the population of Africa and permanently maim hundreds of thousands of children in India with the Polio vaccine. Subsequently, he was instrumental in the development of a strain of Influenza, bioengineering it into the media-promoted "deadly Corona Virus" that is no more deadly than the Common Cold. He formed a partnership with Pfizer and Moderna pharmaceutical laboratories to create a *depopulation* vaccine that could be deployed to eradicate millions of "excess people" throughout the world.

At the commencement of the fake pandemic media blitz, a series of proclamations issued forth from Washington DC and State capitals throughout the nation, warning of the urgent need for the U.S. citizenry to remain sequestered in their homes, wear a mask, maintain social distance, not gather in groups; and the closure of public businesses, retail stores, schools, and community services until further notice. Some commerical enterprises went bankrupt as a result of the shutdown, and millions of Americans were laid off from their jobs; federal stimulus checks were issued to workers who otherwise could not have supported their families. Government propaganda bombarded a captive audience of TV-mesmerized Americans who unquestionly accepted the official narrative of a "Covid Pandemic." The fake news met with no opposition as the hoax was instilled in the minds of over 7 billion people worldwide; the media blitz resulting in a coup of humanity. Because of the almost universal acceptance by the general public of a fabricated "Corona Virus Pandemic," the preposterous farce would perhaps one day never be revealed as "History's Greatest Hoax."

"PEOPLE ARE DYING EVERYWHERE" BUT HOSPITALS ARE VACANT

On October 18, 2019, two months prior to the declared pandemic, at Johns Hopkins University there was a meeting among lower tier globalists to consider the implications of a worldwide contagious disease caused by a viral pathogen. Termed "Event 201" (code name for the year 2021), the so-called "Global Pandemic Exercise" was headed by Bill Gates and funded by his Bill and Melinda Gates Foundation. Among the attendees were leaders from industry, politics and media, all of whom were privy to the advance knowledge that the "exercise" was actually a pre-planned script for what was about to soon transpire, a script that called for a Corona Virus outbreak in Wuhan China. Two months later, in Wuhan China, fake news social contagion spread like an unstoppable virus throughout the world.

In December 2019, a novel viral strain was claimed to have originated at a fish market located 200 yards from one of the world's major biotechnological laboratories in Wuhan. The N–COVID–19 virus was said to affect lung tissue and render its host severely disabled or dead. The media reported that the virus was quickly spreading throughout Europe, and soon thereafter, worldwide. The scripted News constantly updated falsified reports of millions of deaths and the potential for hundreds of millions more. Yet, except for the staged video news clips, there were no collapsed people lying in the streets, no faltering dead bodies wasting away in their homes, and hospitals were curiously empty of lingering dead corpses. What was, and continues to be, going on behind the scenes of the mass delusion?

Internet Article: **CDC: 329 Recorded Deaths So Far Following Experimental COVID mRNA Injections in the U.S.**

January 30, 2021

by Brian Shilhavy

The CDC has done another data dump into the Vaccine Adverse Event Reporting System (VAERS), a U.S. Government funded database that tracks injuries and deaths caused by vaccines.

Search Results

From the 1/22/2021 release of VAERS data:

Found 329 cases where Vaccine is COVID19 and Patient Died

Table		
Age	Count	Percent
< 3 Years	1	0.3%
17-44 Years	7	2.13%
44-65 Years	49	14.89%
65-75 Years	43	13.07%
75+ Years	170	51.67%
Unknown	59	17.93%
TOTAL	329	100%

The data goes through January 22, 2021, with 9,845 recorded adverse events including 329 deaths following injections of the experimental COVID mRNA shots by Pfizer and Moderna.

Over 50% of the deaths are among those over the age of 75.

On the January 15, 2021 data dump, there were 181 deaths following COVID mRNA injections through January 15th. See:

181 Americans Died From COVID-19 Vaccines In Just 2 Weeks, Including Unborn Baby After Mother Took Jab

In the current data dump going through January 22, 2021, there are only two deaths listed between January 15th and January 22nd, VAERS ID 952914 listed on January 18, 2021, and VAERS ID 958809 listed on January 20, 2021.

So 146 of the additional 148 deaths recorded during the past week were from the same time period from the end of December to January 15th—a period of roughly 2 weeks.

That's an average of over 160 deaths a week, so far. How many more deaths will still be recorded during that time period?

As we have previously reported, studies in the past have shown that less than 1% of vaccine injuries are ever reported to the VAERS reporting system.

We are also dependent upon the CDC to supply these statistics.

Earlier this week, it was reported that the VAERS system was "temporarily down." @AlexBerenson tweeted:

So @CDCgov says VAERS went down because it couldn't handle the volume of requests it was getting (this was an email to an academic who asked).

"Starting (Monday) at 7:30 am, the server was overwhelmed by too many incoming queries . . . We are working to resolve this problem."—Alex Berenson (@AlexBerenson) January 26, 2021

So what percentage of all deaths do these 329 recorded represent is currently unknown. It is obviously very significantly higher than 329.

In addition to the 329 deaths out of 9,845 cases of COVID mRNA injuries filed, there were also 722 hospitalizations, over 2000 visits to emergency room doctors, 104 permanent disabilities, and 11 birth defects.

Search Results

From the 1/22/2021 release of VAERS data:

Found 9,845 cases where Vaccine is COVID19

Table

Event Outcome	Count	Percent
Death	329	3.34%
Permanent Disability	104	1.06%
Office Visit	1,219	12.38%
Emergency Room	18	0.18%
Emergency Doctor/Room	2,056	20.88%
Hospitalized	722	7.33%
Recovered	3,870	39.31%
Birth Defect	11	0.11%
Life Threatening	273	2.77%
Not Serious	3,717	37.76%
TOTAL	† 12,319	† 125.13%

† Because some cases have multiple vaccinations and symptoms, a single case can account for multiple entries in this table. This is the reason why the Total Count is greater than 9845 (the number of cases found), and the Total Percentage is greater than 100.

How is this not a national public health crisis? Since these injections are NOT FDA approved and are still experimental, why are they continuing to inject people?

Follow up status on CDC reported Covid deaths: as of February 6, 2021, two-weeks after the above figures were posted, the death toll is now at 500, a 52 percent increase in just 15 days. This *under-reported* figure represents exponential growth; the numbers are actually much higher and will continue to skyrocket. Deaths from the vaccine are being recorded as "Covid Deaths" (ref. below Article from Death Certificate Clerk whistleblower).

According to the CDC None of These Deaths were Caused by the Vaccines (i.e. injections, since the COVID mRNA technology is not a vaccine)

It is well known now that due to federal funding for COVID in 2020 that **nearly all deaths that occurred in 2020 were recorded as "COVID" deaths,** even in cases where the death occurred by traffic accident, shooting, heart attack, etc.

So while there was a huge number of deaths recorded as being caused by COVID in 2020, nearly all other traditional causes of death, such as cancer, heart disease, etc. decreased, so that the total deaths in 2020 will end up being about the same as previous years.

Where is the pandemic? Total Deaths In 2020 Are NO DIFFERENT Than Prior Years

Now we are seeing the exact opposite happen with the rollout of the COVID experimental injections. NONE of them are being recorded as vaccine deaths. Why?

Because the CDC does not provide a category for "vaccine deaths" to be used on death certificates.

To learn more about this, see an article we published in 2018 from a Death Certificate Clerk whistleblower who revealed the politics behind listing "cause of death" on death certificates.

She wrote:

Our current system for capturing mortality rates can and does provide a mostly uninvestigated and inaccurate picture of what causes a death.

The process for creating and registering causes of death for public records is a complicated, convoluted, politicized, completely open to both ignorance and the manipulations of personal, professional, and governmental interests.

I'm the one creating these statistics and I offer you this: If you take one thing away from this, take away a healthier skepticism about even the most accepted mainstream, nationally reported, CDC or other 'scientific' statistics.

What most people don't know is that doctors are not allowed to attest to anything that is not a strictly NATURAL cause of death. (Full article)

When you control the data, you can easily spin it to pretty much say whatever you want it to say, and the CDC is a master at this.

So while the new experimental COVID mRNA injections are rolled here at the beginning of 2021, the deaths that these injections are causing are almost all being recorded as "COVID deaths," using the faulty COVID tests (all of these tests were also fast-tracked by the FDA to get them into the market, by the way) to justify their number.

The CDC is currently in full propaganda mode trying to convince the public that all these deaths and injuries following the injections are "normal," and "expected."

In 2020 there were 2 million *fewer deaths* in the U.S. caused by a biological agent than by the alledged C–19 virus purported to be at large during that same period. The fake reporting of the incidence of Covid–19 *virus* deaths should be transferred to the unofficial real deaths caused by Covid-19 *vaccines* (ref. Section "Covid Disinformation). The only demographic impacted by the Flu (renamed Covid–19) is the weak, frail, immuno-compromised elderly, who typically succumb to Covid Flu-like symptoms (i.e. the Common Cold) every Flu Season. The young, middle-aged demographic are not affected.

THE CORONA VIRUS "PLANDEMIC"

Imagine that somewhere in the world there is a faceless government human drone sitting at a desk, fabricating a steady stream of ludicrous stories about an imaginary pandemic, and that are daily feed to news wire services for posting on the Google-cencored Internet, broadcasted on TV fake news, and printed in Illuminati-controlled newpapers everywhere. He is paid to lie, to make up nonexistent scenarios, with the intent of inciting and perpetrating the greatest hoax in the history of the world. (Such people actually do exist and are employed full-time by corporations. With the job title of "Disinformation Agent," they are paid to lie and create falsehoods to mislead the competition.)

The media-driven pandemic was conceived and outlined in detail many years in advance to cause a worldwide shutdown of all public sectors, services, businesses, and other venues formerly open to a system of free enterprise. This was achieved by the deployment of weaponized news, falsified science, complicit medical community, and a concerted media psychological warfare assault upon all the people of the world. The objectives are to seize control of the global Hive Mind, collapse the world economy, mass sterialization to depopulate, change the human genome, create a cashless world currency, Digital ID, universal vaccinations, ubiquitous citizen surveillance, connecting everyone on the planet to an Artificial Intelligence WiFi grid, and a restructuring of the social order into a caste system of worldwide Socialism. This, "The Great Reset," the "New Normal," is expected to culminate in a globally centralized government with dictatorial control over a vaccinated, microchipped, surveillanced world population that has been reduced by 95 percent of present levels (7.5 billion). The Globalist's Agenda End Game would accomplish all this, and, if successful, the elite controllers would then command from a position of maximum people control upon merging with the world of AI nanotechnology.

COVID DISINFORMATION

The daily assault upon the sensibilities of the world's people by the fake news controlled media would be laughable were it not for the dire consequences. A recent Internet news source reported: *"Bodies Pile Up at crematorium in Germany's virus hot spot,"* is comical to the extreme when considering that the *fabricated story* was intended as disinformation to deceive an undiscerning public into believing that a pandemic exists, when the true purpose of the media fraud is to "convince" the misinformed masses of the urgent need for vaccinations and government social controls "to stop the spread of Corona

Virus." A rabid media blitz has been ongoing since the inception of the manufactured pandemic (March 2020), and even though there is no verifiable nongovernment-funded scientific proof of the hyperbolic claims, yet billions of people in the world believe every word of the Covid deception and are eager to be injected with a *biowarfare vaccine* in order to "Stay Safe." The willingness to believe a lie is a tragedy of the human condition and portends of a bleak future for those so predisposed. It is a future which plays directly into the hands of fiendish billionaire psychopaths who are manipulated and controlled by malevolent spirit beings.

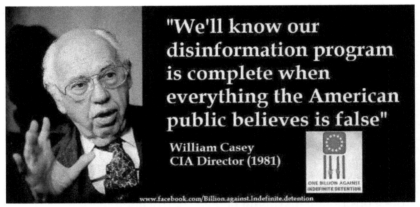

"We'll know our disinformation program is complete when everything the American public believes is false"

William Casey
CIA Director (1981)

ONE BILLION AGAINST
INDEFINITE DETENTION

www.facebook.com/Billion.against.Indefinite.detention

The most effective people-control tool of the globalists is deceit.

Typically, as the lie begins to be exposed to certain individuals and groups, the Shadow Government (supra-government) will commence with "damage control" by circulating more disinformation in an attempt to cover up the original lie. Cover stories will start to come out on the mainstream media news (and on Google searches, social media, YouTube, etc.) which serve as a plausible explanation to "defuse" any potential for a citizen backlash. The propaganda piece will contain partial truth, but the overall intent and effect is to deceive and squelch any doubts that the the false and misleading basic premise still holds—e.g. "the pandemic is real, Covid exists, everyone must be vaccinated." Their protocol is to use falsehood to deceive a people who have been mind-controlled for decades to believe whatever they see or hear from the controlled media.

Deceit is implicit of the parameters used for a medical diagnosis of Covid. Testing positive for "Corona Virus" is a near certainty because of a broad spectrum of blood-borne indicators—all present in healthy individuals—and any one of which "confirms" the presence of the invisible C-19 people-control mechanism. Daily fake news of hospitalizations and deaths falsely attributed to Corona Virus continue to rise as the diagnostic criteria encompasses every possible cause of death, including homocides and automobile accidents. That the "pandemic" is a baseless fraud is clearly evident from the massive amount of documentation proving its lack of credibility, an overview of which is presented in this volume. The Agenda to attribute "pandemic" deaths to an alledged virus, when, in fact, such deaths are *the result of vaccinations* is the highest order of deceit. The Covid bioweapon vaccine is the objective of the fake pandemic.

Throughout 2020 and to the present time, in the months following the commencement of the "invisible enemy" ploy, nearly all deaths were reported as being due to "Covid." This false reporting is used as justification to warrant loss of freedom and liberty for everyone in the world. The charade is daily maintained by fear tactic news stories on the Internet, TV, newspapers, all contributing to a group contagion that has "gone viral." The claim of an "unstoppable pandemic" has nothing to do with any supposed infectious viral agent that is being utilized as a pretense to warrant biowarfare vaccines for *depopulation*.

Upon mass inoculation for the nonexistent viral threat, nothing will change in terms of personal safety and safeguarding public health, and all the restrictions and loss of freedom *will continue to be in full force*. The following is a list of what to expect from the Covid vaccine Agenda.

The Covid vaccine will not:

✓ provide immunity

✓ eliminate the virus

✓ prevent death

✓ guarantee that you will not become infected with Covid–19

✓ make others less susceptible to the virus

✓ eliminate travel ban restrictions

✓ eliminate business closures

✓ eliminate the requirement for home quarantines and lockdowns

✓ eliminate the mandate to wear a mask

Therefore, C–19 vaccines are the objective of a fake pandemic and is shown to be a decoy for people-control in order to bring about the globalist's End Game.

Internet Article: **Why is the CDC Withholding Critical Covid-19 Vaccine Safety Data from the Public?**
February 6, 2021
by Lance D Johnson
The Centers for Disease Control (CDC) is using a passive surveillance system to monitor for vaccine injury during the aggressive covid-19 vaccine rollout.

According to previous CDC studies, this passive surveillance system, the Vaccine Adverse Event Reporting System, (VAERS) captures fewer than 1 percent of vaccine injuries.

To make matters worse, these serious injuries are reported weeks, and many times, months after the vaccine injury occurred. The data coming in to the CDC is not current.

The CDC is using this passive surveillance system to minimize the relevance of vaccine injury, and to promote vaccine injury as a rare occurrence.

In this way, the CDC is manipulating the data to make vaccine injury seem minuscule compared to complications from a naturally-acquired infection.

Study: CDC Broke Federal Law By Manipulating COVID-19 Death Statistics

CDC is under-reporting covid-19 vaccine safety data on anaphylaxis and other allergic reactions

Never before have so many vaccine doses been administered so quickly. By the time vaccine injury data makes it to VAERS, many millions more doses have been administered, including thousands of more injuries.

Consequentially, the CDC's vaccine recommendations are based on weeks-old data that may hide over 99 percent of vaccine injuries.

The CDC is using VAERS to intentionally conceal vaccine injury rates in real time, to embellish public perception of vaccine safety so they can push millions of doses into people's arms. This lackadaisical approach to vaccine safety caused a real-life problem in California. On January 13, California health officials put a hold on 330,000 doses of Moderna's covid-19 vaccine.

The vaccine clinic at the San Diego Petco park stadium reported a cluster of allergic reactions to Moderna's vaccine. The issue prompted the CDC to release a Morbidity Mortality Weekly report on Moderna's covid-19 vaccine.

The CDC pulled data from VAERS that was obtained weeks before, between Dec 21, 2020 and Jan 10, 2021. The report put a spotlight on anaphylaxis, a life-threatening allergic reaction following Moderna's covid-19 vaccine.

After this health issue was brought up and analyzed, the CDC allowed California health officials to go forward and re-release the 330,000 doses of Moderna's vaccine anyway.

The VAERS report did find that anaphylaxis was associated with Moderna's vaccine, but the CDC decided the adverse event was not occurring at an alarming rate.

Even though the VAERS data on anaphylaxis was already under-reported, the CDC had to remove up to 90 percent of the cases to meet the Brighton criteria for anaphylaxis.

Despite the anaphylaxis rate being `diluted by 90 percent, the CDC gave the green light on the Moderna vaccine even though the distorted anaphylaxis rate was still double the accepted average rate for vaccination!

By the third week of January 2021, VAERS had reported 329 deaths and nearly 10,000 other injuries, a small sample of the total damage being done to the population.

CDC withholding vaccine injury data from the public

These vaccine injuries in the VAERS database are not adequately addressed or extrapolated to make up for widespread data reporting errors that are a result of relying on passive vaccine injury surveillance systems.

Many vaccine injuries in the elderly population are omitted from the database due to rigged hospital coding systems; likewise, self-reporting of vaccine injury is often discouraged or goes unheard. Many doctors do not look for vaccine injury or report it because they do not believe it is real.

The CDC is now telling the public that fever, chills, profuse sweating, aches and fatigue after vaccination is the result of the individual's immune system. This is now the alibi to cover up the severity of vaccine injury: Victims are told that their own immune system caused the vaccine injury.

Instead of using vague VAERS data to conceal widespread vaccine injury, the CDC could be using real-time reporting systems that more effectively monitor the damage caused by these vaccines.

The CDC could be pulling more vaccine safety data from the Vaccine Safety Datalink (VSD), a system the agency already manages. They could also pull data from the V-safe database, a system that was specifically created to assess the safety of covid-19 vaccines.

The V-safe database prompts vaccine recipients to report any side effects directly using a cell phone app.

Instead of using this critical data, the CDC decides to go vague, reporting on less than 1 percent of the vaccine injuries, while providing weeks-old reports that they disregard no matter how prevalent the vaccine injury.

Strangely enough, these two, more accurate systems of surveillance are kept private by the CDC; their content is not available for public scrutiny.

As such, the CDC has become a danger to comprehensive informed consent, as the public is coerced to line up and take experimental gene therapy inoculations, no matter the cost to their personal health.

The CDC, a for-profit corporation that is not a government agency, is under the control of the United Nations, a depopulation organization. An independent *vaccine company* with over 20 vaccine patents and $4.6 billion in annual sales, its "service" to the public is to circulate disinformation and vaccine propaganda. CDC data and research is provided by the eugenic globalists, not private sector researchers and laboratories.

DECODING THE GLOBALIST'S DOUBLE-SPEAK

The following statements were posted on the Internet daily list of top news stories as provided by the Rothschild-owned news wire services (e.g. AP, UPI, Reuters), and deal with the media-promoted Covid fake pandemic. The top 10 daily stories are crafted by Rothschild agents and circulated to all media forums—TV, Internet, Newspapers, etc. Keep this in mind when reading the following ridiculously ludicrous disinformation. Decoded interpretations are in brackets.

"Austria extends lockdown to Feb 7, toughens some measures"
[Forced citizen home imprisonment prevents the possibility of an organized revolt.]

"At G-7, UK says world must act as one in virus vaccine push"
[The "push" is not for vaccine consensus, but rather for unifying the governments and people of the world under a "One World" totalitarian system of Orwellian control.]

"State leaders ponder tougher virus rules"
[More lockdowns, more quarantines, more social distancing . . . because the citizenry is becoming suspicious of the lies.]

"Dutch propose curfew to rein in virus; will ban more flights. Lawmakers back coronavirus curfew despite criticism"
[The true agenda is not virus control, but people control.]

"Portugal sets record in one of world's worst virus surges; leads in average virus cases per capita"
[National leaders are fully "on board" with the pandemic farce; in obedience to their globalist masters they cooperate with reporting false statistics.]

"Hard-hit Czech Republic reaches 1 million confirmed cases"
[The criteria used to determine "confirmed" cases are biological markers found in all healthy disease-free people. "Confirmed" Covid includes symptomologies of the Common Cold.]

"French Riviera cities under lockdown as new infections soar"
["New infections" and "Variants" provide a never-ending lockdown scenario.]

"Vaccine skepticism hurts East European anti-virus efforts. . . talk of coming civil war"

"EU insists virus shots will remain voluntary"
[This was posted the day following the previous statement, and was "damage control" to minimize potential civil unrest and resistance.]

"Spain's rising cases [of C-19] give pandemic hospital a second chance"
["Pandemic Hospital"—inventing terminology to support the Covid lie. Hospital "Corona Virus Wards" are curiously devoid of patients.]

"UK aims to give 1st COVID-19 shot to all adults by September"
[Pre-emptive Programming: mandatory vaccine death shots are coming. Get ready.]

"The Latest: Swiss quarantine 2 hotels over the new virus variant"
[An unending series of imaginary "variants" insures that the fake pandemic will continue to terrorize indefinitely.]

"China; WHO should have acted quicker to stop pandemic"
[Retro-active "review" for instilling fear of future government tyranny.]

"Government of Czechoslovakia must build more crematoriums to handle COVID deaths"
[Disinformation to spread the falsehood of "dead bodies," when in fact there are no dead bodies to cremate.]

"EU commission urges member states to speed up vaccinations"
[Before the Sheeple realize that it's a hoax and they are experimental vaccine victims.]

"UK chief says new virus variant may be more deadly
Stay Home—Protect The NHS—Save Lives"
[Constant fear and trauma to induce compliance: "Don't leave your house, watch TV, don't think, believe everything you hear about Corona Virus. . ."]

"Virus variant from South Africa detected in US for 1st time. S. Africa virus variant found in S. Carolina"

["Variants" (mutations) are a false pretense to justify ongoing vaccinations. If there actually were any "variants" they would be bioengineered in a vaccine laboratory.]

"UK doctors seek review of 12-week gap between vaccine doses"

[The globalist's are planning for more than one vaccine.]

"German virus death toll tops 50,000 even as infections sink"

[Undocumented claims of deaths caused by a nonexistent scourge is an effective decoy for citizen control and to mandate vaccinations. Compare this statement to that below.]

"Korea has zero reported C –19 cases, but wants vaccine"

[The fake pandemic is mandated for all nations by the globalist's supra-government under the threat of sanctions; no country is exempt from depopulation vaccines.]

"UK vaccination drive expands as virus toll nears 100,000"

[According to this figure, 600 among every 100,000 people in UK have recently died from a nonexistent cause (UK population: 67 million). The pre-Covid death rate in UK was 900 per 100,000. So, 300 *fewer* people have died as a result of the fake pandemic.]

"Dutch police clash with anti-lockdown protesters in 2 cities; condemn rioting over virus curfew, fear more violence"

[Predictive Programming: conditioning the Sheeple not to protest.]

"Russia leaders to discuss vaccine supply"

[The fake pandemic is a global operation directed by Illuminati crime families. The leadership of all nations are heavily infiltrated with globalists having a depopulation agenda. No countries are exempt from promoting the Covid deception.]

"EU poses more travel restrictions to stop virus variants"
[All means of evading the pandemic madess are blocked; cannot flee to remote areas of the world to escape it.]

"UK's 'tsunami' of grief as coronavirus deaths pass 100,000"
[This post included an image of an elderly couple in their 90's. Death's from seasonal influenza in 2019 surpassed deaths falsely attributed to Corona Virus during the same period. The elderly's weak immune system predisposes them to succumbing to common ailments such as the seasonal "Flu," (the Common Cold) which, for young and middle-aged people, does not result in death. Starting in 2020, to inflate "deaths by Covid," the Flu has been renamed "Corona Virus."]

"EU regulator authorizes AstraZenca vaccine for all adults"
"Study: Russia's Sputnik V vaccine appears safe, effective"
[Next generation of fake pandemic bioweaponized vaccines.]

"Experts notice pandemic's mental health toll on German youth"
[Induced stress caused by forced compliance with Covid restrictions, 5G radiation from cell towers and Starlink, as well as constantly reinforced paranoia, will continue to be detrimental to the psychological health of everyone, and especially children.]

"UK says new study vindicates delaying 2nd virus vaccine shot"
[Fake pandemic inoculations will not end with the initial Covid vaccine, and there will be an on-going series of "variant pandemics" requiring injection of more biowarfare death shots. These variant vaccines are Part 2 of a binary vaccine, causing death.]

Portugal scrambles for virus beds; health system threatened"
[More fear. But there are no dead bodies for the extra virus beds.]

"UN to rich nations: Don't undermine COVAX vaccine program"
[Obey your genocidal Illuminati masters, or else.]

"AstraZeneca vaccine being tweaked to fight S. Africa variant"
[Inventing a never-ending series of "variants" allows the pandemic fraud to perpetuate indefinitely; it will never be over.]

"UK tests house-to-house in hunt for new Covid-19 variant"
[Pseudo-rationale for escalating tyranny. In America, HR6666 gives police the right to storm homes and remove family members suspected of Covid. No one and no where is safe from the tyranny of a criminal government.]

"Some school leaders are not assuming Fall reopening"
[A control mechanism to disrupt the educational process; young children traumatized, school lessons transmitted through 5G radiation-emitting computers, encouraging social isolation, decreased quality of education.]

"EU to double COVAX vaccine funding to 1 billion Euros"
[More efficient global access to bioweaponized vaccines and fabricated data to facilitate perpetuation of the pandemic hoax. 'COVID' changed to 'COVAX' in order to make Corona Virus synonymous with the vaccine.]

"UK: poorer nations should get 'gold standard' COVAX vaccines"
[Third world "poorer" nations are a primary target for depopulation. Biochemical parameters of weaponized C-19 vaccines are ethnically adjusted to maximize damage.]

"UNICEF asking for speedy transport of vaccines"
[Hurry and deliver the toxic death shots! The Sheeple are beginning to wake up!]

"Around the globe virus cancels Spring travel for millions"
[With continued restrictions and deprivations, it begs the question: At what point will the Sheeple finally say "No" to the overbearing tyranny? . . . The answer is: "Never."]

"Southern California variant has spread to 19 States"
[There is no limit to this theme. The New Normal requires "variants" and a "rising death toll" that is actually caused by the vaccine, not the alledged virus.]

"Texas confirms 227 more confirmed Covid-19 deaths"
[227 more elderly people died from the seasonal Flu that was renamed "Covid-19.]

"Dutch opposition lawmakers back new coronavirus curfew laws"
[Stay in your houses! Citizens got guns and might use them, on us.]

"Portugal's relief at falling Covid-19 cases tempered by fear"
["Fear," it works, every time.]

"Canada clears Johnson & Johnson vaccine"
[More vaccine companies competing for "death shot" business.]

"Turkish vaccine teams target isolated villages"
[Total geographic penetration. The globalist's are determined no one escapes tyranny.]

"Germany limits travel from French region over virus variants"
[Travel restirictions contain citizen movement which facilitates Covid tracking.]

"Anti-vax at the Vatican? You might lose your job"
[Catholic Pope/Vatican is part of the globalist's Illuminati cabal.]

"Serbia welcomes AstraZenca vaccine shipment"
[The proverbial Trojan Horse.]

""EU hails deals to get more vaccine shots, tackle variants"
[Playing the never-ending "Variant" card.]

"Alarm grows in Serbia over virus surge; lockdown urged"
[The response to fake "virus surge" is urgent "people-control" (lockdown, restrictions).]

"Europe staggers as infectious variants power virus surge"
["Variants" will be a continual justification for more deadly vaccines.]

"Hungary closes businesses as cases, deaths rise"
[The predictable cycle is: fear, business shutdowns/quarantines, vaccines, lessening of fear, "variants," more fear, more vaccines, more buisiness shutdowns/quarantines . . .]

"EU nations have received 18.5 million Covid-19 vaccines"
[The culling of humanity has begun.]

Plus more propaganda every day . . .

What do the above statements have in common?
They are all lies. On a daily basis many similar fabricated scenarios are sent from the globalist Illuminati crime families to their news wire services and Google for posting on the Internet to instill fear and compliance with Covid bioterrorism. None of the media statements contain a shred of truth and are all designed to maintain the world's citizenry in a constant state of anxiety and trauma-induced fear in order to control their behavior, insure compliance with vaccinations, and serve as pre-emptive programming to prepare them for the tyranny to come. Continuous media-promoted disinformation, uncritically accepted as irrefutable truth by the Sheeple, is essential for indoctrinating the world masses with the Covid deception.

... and Sheeple all over the world believe every word of it.

In Orwell's *1984,* there is a perpetual war between *Oceania, Eurasia* and *Eastasia,* the prevailing global superstates at the time of a dehumanizing ultra-surveillance dystopian society. Fabricated media reports of conflicts between these countries (the enemy nations may not have even existed) induced the citizenry to regard the combative societies with a sense of irrational fear and hatred toward an "invisible enemy" that unified them in a common purpose to serve "Big Brother." The above news stories accomplish the same psychological effect; the "invisible enemy" tactic is a standard protocol which has been deployed by despotic governments throughout modern history.

When the globalist's were ready to spring their pandemic farce on the world and in America, the entire country was put on ready alert—masks required to be worn and social distancing to be observed in all public areas "to stop the spread of Corona Virus." Everywhere, people complied without question or voicing doubt that the government news was a reflection of reality. The Center

for Disease Control (CDC)—a nongovernment agency that is a vaccine company which owns over 20 vaccine patents and sells $4.6
billion of vaccines per year; and the World Health Organization
(WHO)—a globalist front for promoting government health-related
disinformation, continue to report a steadily rising Covid death toll
throughout the world. (Both groups are UN agencies; the United
Nations is a propaganda tool of the globalists depopulation Agenda.)
Person-to-person contact was now discouraged; everyone subject
to an undeclared Martial Law quarantine and commanded to remain
sequestered in their home where they feared for their lives while
watching the government-controlled news on their TV's that programmed them to believe in a "deadly pandemic." (The globalist's
borrowed this idea of an ever-present big screen TV monitor from
Orwell's revealing novel, published in 1949.) As soon as the news
propaganda was launched, people lost contact with reality, their
world collapsing into trite cliches, baseless rumors, TV mantras and
the parroting of fake news reports devoid of any substantive truth.
Their only "truth" was that which they saw and heard on televised
"programming" and Internet-censored Google. They were easily controlled and believed the global fantasy that had been planned years
in advance. Throughout the world more than 7 billion people and
325 million Americans voluntarily remained in their homes, sitting
before a glowing mind-control device, where they are monitored
while passively absorbing a constant stream of the most ludicrious
falsehoods ever conceived by a criminal government. The stage was
now set for the second phase of launching a massive genocidal campaign upon humanity, one that would exceed anything the world
has ever known—*Vaccines*, weaponized to trace, track, alter DNA,
Neuralink, and subsequently kill the recipient.

"WE'RE ALL IN THIS TOGETHER"

Shortly after the announcement of the media-promoted fake pandemic and government-mandated home quarantines, the escalating
hysteria among the world masses was pacified by simplistic slogans

like, "We're all in this together," "Stay Safe," and the "New Normal." Redefining what is "normal" served as a powerful psychological mechanism to shift the people's focus away from the problem and toward the blind acceptance of a dramatically changed lifestyle that consists of a locked-down society of masked, separated, vaccinated, freightened, noncritical-thinking, media-controlled global citizens. Consequently, upon acceptance of the collossal lie, an abberration became the standard model for dictating human behavior. People the world over soon adapted to the "New Normal" of wearing a mask (conditioned by media programming to believe was "chic" and "fashionable"), remaining six feet apart from others, and spending most of their time fearful of their own shadow, without any social contact. Those few who did not comply with the government demands for conformity were viewed by the mind-controlled major-ity as "contagious," "dangerous," "conspiracy theorists." Suddenly, a rational-thinking person had no place in a culture that exhibited schitzophrenic behavior upon wearing disease-promoting masks to stop the spread of a nonexistent airbone viral pathogen. Reduction of their ability to reason was perhaps due to the re-breathed toxic CO_2 and reduced intake of oxygen, resulting in a cognitive deficit in brain neurons and consequent limited awareness from a lowering of intelligence. This would account for a lack of protest as the Covid psychosis manifested as widespread global insanity.

An entire world society dances to the tune of a planetary elite class tightening the net which enslaves them with each passing decree. Today it is wearing a mask and keeping your social distance; tomorrow it will be to line up and submit to an injection of a vac-cine containing lethal ingredients, and that will track you, alter your DNA, transfer delayed onset stealth diseases, erase your Free Will, and determine your eternal destiny. The planned people-control strategy has so far worked perfectly, and very few (the Elect, Saved) can see through the massive deception and silently "opt out." Even fewer suspect they are a herd of cowered Sheeple being led to the slaughter.

Masks do not prevent disease, they proliferate disease, resulting in respiratory illnesses from inhalation of wearer's own CO_2, impeded intake of O_2, causing hypoxia and subsequent cognitive dysfunction; and concentration of pathogenic disease vectors trapped in the moisture-retaining material.

The people/sheeple were told to wear a mask, and obeyed without question. Never did they consider that the .01 micron-sized virus could easily pass through a cloth mesh of 10–20 microns, which is 1000 to 2000 times larger than the presumed virus. And even though the mask habors pathogens, restricts their breathing, concentrates re-breathed toxic CO_2 (400%), and reduces their intake of oxygen, creating a low O_2 concentration in their venous blood—which destroys brain cells and enhances the proliferation of anerobic pathogens—they did not protest the requirement to wear a useless disease-promoting mask. (There exists the possibility that the masks have been deliberately inoculated with an Influenza pathogen.) Neither did they object to "Social Distancing," remaining six feet apart to "stop the spread of Covid." It never occurred to them that the presumed C–19 malfactor, if truly present in an enclosed space, would be uniformly saturated throughout a room and would thus reveal the spacing requirement to serve some other purpose, which, of course, is to inhibit the gathering of like minds and prevent a citizen uprising against the Covid elites. (Satelite imaging surveillance provides a clearer "body count" when the "target species" is not close together. A distance of six feet or more shows up on monitors as a single individual.)

It is a violation of the Constitution for any State Govenor to demand the wearing of masks. Govenor's are not law makers; they cannot legislate new laws, but may only make recommendations and execute existing laws. Therefore, any demand by a State representative for the public to wear masks is prohibited by law and puts the citizenry in servitude to the government—i.e. slavery, which is yet another violation of the Constitution. A medical license is required in order to propose or mandate such a measure, and even then, it is not law. State executive officials typically do not hold a medical degree.

The author recommends claiming a "medical exemption" whenever approached by an employee of an establishment seeking to demand the wearing of a mask in order to allow entry. Upon stating, "I have a medical exemption" (issued from God), the antagonist is bound by law to cease and desist, or charges of menancing can be brought against the individual employee and the owner of the facility. Yet, the irrational furvor is not easily quelled, and the belief is so strong that you represent a serious health risk to others that often your legitimate claim will be ignored and you will be commanded to leave the premises or suffer the consequences of arrest for tresspassing. (It is never advisable to engage in logical discussion with someone who is TV-programmed, mind-controlled, has been brainwashed by a satanic culture, lacks the intellectual capacity to make simple deductions, and who is truth-adverse. For someone who has been repeatedly vaccinated as a child, and that has for all their life consumed processed neurotoxic food products and drank fluoridated municipal tap water, your well-reasoned argument will be of no effect.)

9 REASONS WHY COVID IS A LIE

1) Only affects Immuno-deficient elderly.

2) Non-virulent, brief life cycle, does not persist; spike protein is easily denatured and renders the virus nonfunctional.

3) A fake biowarfare pandemic is stated by the Globalist's Agenda.

4) Just as there were no "9/11 Terrorists," there is no "Corona Virus."

5) A naive media-programmed public will accept any media lie.

6) Hospitals are paid for each death falsely reported as "Covid."

7) Seasonal Flu statistics have been transferred to Covid statistics.

8) "Deaths by Covid" are deaths caused by the Covid vaccine.

9) Those who believe a lie, God has given over to believe only lies (2 Thessalonians 2:10–12).

GLOBALIST AGENDAS FOR THE CORONA VIRUS "OUTBREAK"

- Global Digital Identification microchipping (ID 2020): Will enable the world controllers to monitor everyone on the planet.

- Mandatory vaccinations: Serves as an excuse to invade the human body, and uses nanotechnology to insert nonhuman DNA sequences into chromosomes; mass sterialization, GPS satellite tracking by a programmable microchip.

- Martial Law quarantines: Suspension of Constitutional and Civil Rights, no Habeas Corpus (arrest and incarceration without cause).

- Imposed social isolation to prevent group communication and action.

- Ongoing vaccinations: Viral "Variants" used as justification for injecting more gene-splicing genetic material into your body to restructure genetic code and activate binary bioweapon.

- Vaccine chemical and biological toxic components: Delayed-onset stealth diseases for mass extermination.

- Binary vaccine triggers: Future vaccines activate vaccine precursors.

- Global mind-link of human brains en masse to Neuralink implantable brain-machine interface.

- Global surveillance via Starlink 5G satellites and 5G towers.

- HR6666: Allows police to enter citizen's homes under the pretense of testing family members for a nonexistent virus, removing those who test "positive" for C–19, and for them to be quarantined in a FEMA Camp where they will be forcibly vaccinated against their will.

- Business shutdowns and home quarantines to reduce GNP and crash the U.S. and global economies.

- Cashless digital global noncurrency: paper money and other means of financial transactions taken out of circulation. Electronic Credit/Debits for maximizing people control.

- Luminescent biometric tattoo embedded in the back of right hand or forehead: Stores all personal information—medical, financial, political, religious, etc. (Revelation 13:16 Mark of the Beast).

- FEMA incarceration for those who refuse to be vaccinated: Forced vaccine or beheading (Revelation 20:4). At the time of this writing (1/21), residents of New York City are being transported to upState New York FEMA Camps near the Catskill Mountains. All across America, more than 1000 FEMA camps are currently in existence; large fenced-in areas, or permanent buildings, some with gas chambers and guillotines. More Camps can be erected in a brief period of time. Large capacity facilities such as sports stadiums and Walmart stores may also serve as government processing centers for detaining those who refuse to be vaccinated, publicly expose the Covid lie, or warn others to resist vaccination.

The staged Corona Virus outbreak of Spring 2020 was the initial phase of a more ambitious long-term global genocidal/people control project. It served as a "Beta Test" to gauge the reaction of the world's populous and their willingness to comply with totalitarian rule, believe noncredible media falsehoods, and passively submit to dictates that violate their Constitutional/Civil Rights and their God-given freedom. Without protest or struggle, the Sheeple exchanged their liberty for safety from a virus, an invisible enemy that, technically, did not even exist.

WHEN THE COVID VACCINE BECOMES MANDATORY:

- Cannot Buy or Sell without scanned proof of having been vaccinated
- Martial Law/suspension of the Constitution
- Home Quarantines
- Forced Vaccinations
- Changed Human Genetics
- Starlink computer-to-brain interface activated
- Global Tracking
- Constant government supervision and control
- Incurable new diseases and bodily ailments
- Starvation (those who refuse to submit to the vaccine will not be permitted to transact business or hold a job)
- Homelessness
- Jail/FEMA "Re-education/Detention Centers" Death Camps; Torture and Death by poisonous gas, beheading (Rev 20:4)

The Covid lockdown pandemic will continue to be in force for another 30 years (ref. Appendix B). Restrictions will never be lifted; society will never go back to the way it was, and you will be a prisoner given a maximum 30 year sentence.

Better learn to accept, and even enjoy, your servitude, because—since you would not stand up and speak out—you have no other choice. At this point, it is too late.

CHAPTER 5

MANDATORY VACCINES, NANOBOTS, MICROCHIPPING, 5G, STARLINK SURVEILLANCE

"Once the herd accepts mandatory forced vaccination, it's game over! They will accept anything—forcible blood or organ donations—'for the greater good.' We can genetically modify children and sterilize them—'for the greater good.' Control Sheep minds and you control the herd. Vaccine makers stand to make billions, and many of you in this room today are investors. It's a big win –win. We thin out the herd and the herd pays us for providing extermination services. Now, what's for lunch, huh?"

—Henry Kissinger, in a speech to the
World Health Organization Council on Eugenics, 2/25/09

At first, the irrational demands are presented as a suggestion. Then, as the numbers of pacified global citizens continue to grow, the suggestion becomes a requirement. Finally, the requirement segues into law, and what was once considered rational and normal suddenly becomes punishable by arrest and imprisonment. It will be a time of a dystopian *1984*, "a time of universal deceit, where speaking the truth is a revolutionary act." And where *good is called evil, and evil is called good* (Isaiah 5:20). As the tyranny escalates, further resistance is met with force, then, finally, incarceration and execution. Imposed restrictions on freedom and liberty are not lifted once the "threat" no longer exists. When psychopaths are in control, nothing will stop their global Agenda.

As detailed in "Global Vaccine Passport will be Required for Travel, The Commons Project," the World Economic Forum and The Rockefeller Foundation have joined forces to create the CommonPass1, a digital "Health Passport" that will be required for travel. Adopted by most or all nations, the Commonpass will eventually integrate with personal health apps such as Apple Health and CommonHealth, and when traveling, an individual's personal health record will be evaluated and compared to a country's entry requirements. If you do not meet them you will be directed to an approved testing and vaccination location.

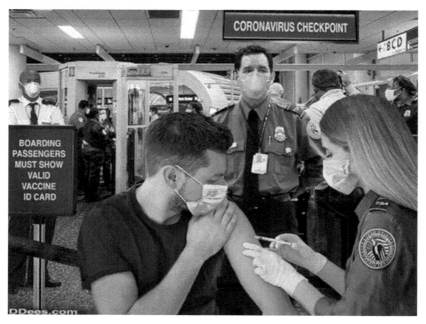

The groundwork for CommonPass was laid out in an April 21, 2020 white paper by The Rockefeller Foundation, which shows that proof of vaccination is part of a *permanent surveillance and social control structure*, one that severely limits personal liberty and freedom of choice. Proof of vaccination status will not become obsolete once the fake pandemic is pronounced over (if ever), since it is integral to the Globalist's Agenda of worldwide surveillance, people control, genetic alteration, and mass sterialization.

A PROPOSAL TO PAY EACH VACCINE RECIPIENT $1500

The suggestion of bribing people to submit to the Covid vaccine bio-weapon was raised by U.S. Representative John Delaney. "The faster we get 75% of this country vaccinated, the faster we end COVID and the sooner everything returns to normal," Delaney told Alabama news site AL.com. "We have to create, in my judgment, an incentive for people to really accelerate their thinking about taking the vaccine." According to noncredible government reports, as of November 2020, about 58 percent of Americans said they will take the vaccine. This figure is inflated and intended as predictive programming. The actual percentage is less than 10 percent. (Just ask around and you will discover that less than 1 in 10 people wish to be vaccinated. Those who desire injection with a gene-splicing neurotoxic tracking device have been brainwashed and are spiritually dead.) According to a November 2020 Lancet paper, between 75% and 90% of the U.S. population would need to be vaccinated in order to achieve what is termed Herd Immunity (a concept that only applies to natural infection, not vaccination). Democratic presidential candidate Andrew Yang and economic adviser N. Gregory Mankiw have made similar propositions, suggesting the government make a $1,000 pandemic stimulus payment contingent upon receipt of a Covid–19 vaccination. But before you acquiesce to the dangling carrot, ask yourself: "How much is my health and my soul worth to me?"

DOWNLOADING AN OPERATING SYSTEM INTO HUMANS

By utilizing weaponized vaccinations Bill Gates is hoping to download an operating system into your body. In the manner of a computer operating system, with vaccines he has plans to program your mind using nanochip technology combined with CrispR gene splicing. The Covid "virus" is the equivalent of the computer virus and will require an "update" vaccine to address the need for combating "variants" and future planned "pandemics."

Gates and the techno-pharma companies are installing a digital interface control grid that links to Microsoft's new $10 billion JEDI cloud at the Department of Defense, and also Amazon's $multi-billion cloud contract for the CIA that is shared with all U.S. intelligence agencies. They are using the term "vaccines" to describe what are actually injectible AI nanotechnology weaponry, invasive surveillance, and microdot-robots.

Self-replicating nanobots introduced into the human body via vaccine hypodermic injection.

Internet Article: **Moderna Admits: mRNA Jabs Are an 'Operating System' Designed to Program Humans**

January 5, 2021

by *Lance D Johnson*

The experimental injections being rolled out by Moderna and Pfizer are nothing similar to traditional vaccines. These mRNA platforms are an "operating system" designed to program human beings and turn their cells into efficient drug delivery systems. Moderna is now going public with the real intentions behind the mRNA platform. The mRNA technology platform is similar to a computer operating system, the company admits.

Scientists prepare a unique mRNA sequence that codes for a specific protein. Once injected into humans, this program is carried out in the individual's body, at the cellular level.

The mRNA platform is where Big Pharma merges with Big Tech, enslaving human beings to a controlling system designed to profit from their cellular and biological functions into the unforeseeable future.

Moderna admits that healthy immune systems are a threat to their mRNA platform

The body can generate its own protection. All it needs is the right information.

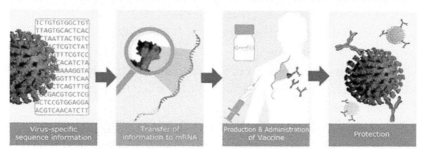

As mRNA platforms go live on human populations, Moderna admits that healthy human immune responses can actually destroy the mRNA sequences before they get into the person's cells.

The immune system may attack the program and its RNA fragments, leading to negative outcomes that could include molecular deficiencies, hormonal defects, etc..

If the protein folding is disrupted, the proteins may never achieve their desired functionality, leading to partial development of antigens that never confer targeted immunity to coronavirus spike proteins.

The body may turn on its own cells in the process, causing hyper-inflammatory responses and autoimmune issues that are the precursor to organ failure and various disease processes.

During the so-called pandemic, public health officials were mum on the actions people should take to mount a healthy immune response to infection. Now we know why these public health officials were telling people they must wait on a vaccine to go back to normal.

The people behind the mRNA experimentation of humans are building psychological justification and scientific precedent to declare human immune systems incapable.

Their first attempt is this: WHO Changes Definition Of 'Herd Immunity', Literally Re-Writing Hundreds Of Years Of Scientific Understanding, Just To Push Vaccines

In this way, people will submit their bodies to the latest mRNA programs as they become dependent on the biological software that have been created for them.

This is an open door toward trans-humanism, and millions of people are buying into it.

By casting shame on human immune systems, drug companies have also found the perfect alibi for when their experiments cause injury in humans.

It's not the injected technology that is causing allergic reactions, seizures, infertility and death, claim the drug companies . . .

It's the individual's human's immune system that is causing all the pain and misery, they demand.

The drug companies will demand that more carefully crafted mRNA programs and interventions will be needed to "perfect" human beings.

The new mRNA vaccines are dependency programs, designed to manipulate and enslave human biological functions

Moderna brags that "several hundred scientists and engineers are solely focused on advancing Moderna's platform technology."

These scientists are attempting to "hack" humans with bio-information and make populations dependent on the technology. Moderna has even dubbed their mRNA platform the 'Software of Life.' These scientists are looking for ways to help the foreign mRNA avoid immune detection. They are also experimenting with ways to trick the cell's ribosomes into processing the mRNA as if it was natural.

Moderna was founded on the success of using modified RNA to reprogram the function of a human stem cell, therefore genetically modifying it.

As these RNA "operating systems" are installed in human bodies, it becomes even more clear that drug companies are looking to genetically modify and own human proteins while controlling biological processes for generations to come.

On both a psychological and physiological level, human beings are being branded like cattle as they submit to these mRNA software programs. **This system is not medicine, nor is it vaccination.** This system is complete cellular manipulation, using foreign biological molecules to code, decode, regulate, change the expression of, and alter the physiological instructions within human beings.

COVID VACCINE IS BIOTERRORISM, NOT MEDICINE

Today's vaccines are not medicine, they are a concoction of toxic chemical elements and bioengineered nanotechnological gene-altering DNA-splicing components. The reason why these revelations may come as a surprise even to the somewhat well-informed is because of media censorship to supress the truth about the dangers of techno-weaponized vaccines. To prevent exposure of the truth about vaccines, all media forums are regulated by the globalist's; the Internet is the domain of Google, a globalist front for controlling the flow of information availability to the public. Hence, a massive disinformation campaign exists to discourage further investigation and inquiry.

The Covid Vaccine, and all subsequent fake pandemic vaccines—including a soon to be introduced *cancer vaccine*—are the most devious way to introduce nanobots into the bloodstream that can later be activated by a trigger such as another vaccine (or some other factor, such as a 5G frequency transmission). Orbiting Starlink satellites, 5G cell towers, and Contact Tracing of vaccine injectees will enable seemless access to every vaccinated person on the planet for accessing their programming. The globalist's want 24/7 direct access to your body, and they will accomplish it by mandatory vaccines that contain a microdot to trace, track, and link you to the global Starlink 5G electromagnetic grid. The global madman's expressed urgent need for universal vaccinations is predicated upon microchipping the world population for enabling human linkage with microwave and radio wireless signals broadcast from cell towers and from over 50,000 SpaceX, Amazon, and AT&T satellites in orbit around the Earth. They expect this objective to be accomplished by the year 2030. Additonally, there are other goals to be attained by global vaccinations, specifically, gene-splicing the human genome for mass sterialization (3 generations), and to permanently alter mankind's genetics from human to nonhuman. Fake pandemic bioweaponized vaccines contain a programmable microchip linked to quantum computers (Neuralink). The microdot chip is also a downloadable GPS tracking device that will contain a dossier of financial, medical, and other identifying data about the recipient. The mRNA vaccine concoction includes components of nonhuman DNA—part living organic, part non-living inorganic machine—which can splice into chromosomes to alter an individual's genetic makeup.

Unknown to all but a small minority among the world's population, the vaccine agenda is not intended for medicinal purposes, and has absolutely nothing whatsoever to do with preventing disease. Rather, it is a calculated attempt to control people and depopulate the planet. The chemical ingredients of a vaccine are neurotoxic and intended to cause severe reactions in a large percentage of those who submit to it; the initial adverse immune reaction can be fatal.

The fake Covid "Pandemic" launched by the international elites in 2020 provided a pretense to justify global vaccinations for tracing, tracking, and controlling the citizenry, and for depopulating the planet by vaccine injury and premature death. Mandatory vaccines will become a never-ending dependency scenario which they will

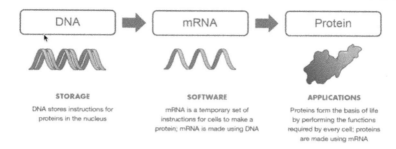

STORAGE	SOFTWARE	APPLICATIONS
DNA stores instructions for proteins in the nucleus	mRNA is a temporary set of instructions for cells to make a protein; mRNA is made using DNA	Proteins form the basis of life by performing the functions required by every cell; proteins are made using mRNA

Our mRNA Medicines – The 'Software of Life'

When we have a concept for a new mRNA medicine and begin research, fundamental components are already in place.

Generally, the only thing that changes from one potential mRNA medicine to another is the coding region – the actual genetic code that instructs ribosomes to make protein. Utilizing these instruction sets gives our investigational mRNA medicines a software-like quality. We also have the ability to combine different mRNA sequences encoding for different proteins in a single mRNA investigational medicine.

We are leveraging the flexibility afforded by our platform and the fundamental role mRNA plays in protein synthesis to pursue mRNA medicines for a broad spectrum of diseases.

The new mRNA vaccines are "dependancy programs" that instruct human cells to produce artificial proteins. Once the individual's genetic code has been breached and the cell's reproductive machinery has been hijacked, natural immunity is permanently disabled, requiring more injections of biowarfare vaccines which do not confer immunity, but replicate the disease pathogen.

utilize for injecting nanotechnological weaponry into people in order to lower the threshold of their cognitive awareness, and also as a means of extermination. (Bill Gates, the most prolific serial killer in the history of the world, prior to the fake Covid pandemic, had already killed 100 million people in Africa under the pretense of a vaccine disease preventative. He is a major driving force behind the Covid and other fake pandemic vaccines.)

Corona Virus is an excuse for the invasion of the human body with nonotech components that reprogram human genetics and link to the AI Cloud WiFi Neuralink planetary control grid. C–19 is reported to have already "mutated" (variants) and will require more nanotechnology vaccine injections, with more foreign protein gene-spliced sequences to be inserted into or deleted from the human genome. (The variant "report" may be disinformation, and variants may not actually exist, just as C–19 does not actually exist in the technical sense of a "deadly" Virus. For decades, Corona Virus has been a causal agent for the seasonal Flu/Common Cold.)

The global transformation will be completed when the human race is transformed into a nonhuman race. Until that time, there will be a continuous series of planned and scripted "pandemics," such as SPARS, scheduled to start in 2025 and last until 2028. More vaccines, more injected nanochips, more disabling immune-response gene splicing. It will be an ongoing planned script of weaponized injections, close supervision and control by government; a nightmarish perpetual lockdown quarantine of terrorized, freightened, sequestered, "Hunger Games" isolated communities comprised of obedient, mask-wearing, sterile, disinfected, sanitized, reduced IQ, unquestioning half-human New World Order souless zombies. This is the Globalist's Agenda End Game. The "New Normal" is to acquiesce, to obey, and to die believing the Covid fake pandemic lie. At no point did the people of planet earth protest or resist, and, in the process, they forfeited not only their freedom and their humanity, but also their very soul.

Predictive (Pre-emptive) programming is the globalist's planned script for the future of humanity. Hollywood is their projection screen for conditioning the global masses to the world of robotized, microchipped, Neura-linked, genetically-altered, soul-dead zombies. The Globalist's End Game is the ultimate rebellion against God.

The globalist's objective is domination of the world's people—mind, body and soul. The technology to achieve this goal is readily available, in place, and currently being implemented upon an unsuspecting world population. It will continue to advance until those remaining alive among humankind are gene-spliced and mind-linked to the AI Cloud for the creation of a planetary Hive Mind directed by quantum computers. The staged Covid pandemic is an integral component of the "Great Reset" to obliterate any vestige of the characteristics that define the human race. Mankind will be transformed into a Godless society of vaccinated nonhuman cyborgs linked to Artificial Intelligence; man will change from being created in the image and likeness of God, to being bioengineered into the image of Lucifer/Satan.

THE BRAVE NEW WORLD ORDER

In the Brave New World globalist's End Game of a worldwide dictatorial government modeled after China's Orwellian social credit system, millions of surveillance cameras and brainwashed citizen spies insure compliance with a multitude of petty government rules and regulations; a lock down world society, digitized economy, and nanotechnological infrastructure for tracing, tracking, vaccinating and microchipping the entire human race.

Since the "outbreak" of Covid–19 outside of China, the World Health Organization has taken a prominent role in "handling the pandemic" on a global scale. The unquestioned power and influence of this nongovernment organization, created by the UN, is in control of directing governments throughout the world to conform their approach to a pandemic response according to the WHO's guidelines. From this it is evident that the globalist's are directing world events from behind the scenes and are using a global entity to bypass any democratic process. Director General of the WHO, Tedros Adhanon Ghebreyesus, recently stated that after a year of having declared a global pandemic crisis, the organization "is still struggling to keep on top of the evolving science of Covid-19." What he means by "evolving science" is the manufactured threat of viral variants, which are merely a convenient excuse to further the vaccine depopulation Agenda.

As the medical propaganda arm of the globalists, the WHO is in the business of disseminating false health reports and issuing directives to form citizen opinions worldwide in order to create a consensus of compliance upon large segments of the global population. This UN entity falsely reports the number of Corona Virus cases when claiming millions of deaths, none of which are subject to third party verification. The WHO (medical propaganda) and the FDA (a front for pharmaceutical companies), and the CDC (a vaccine company), are effective means utilized by the global controllers for pushing the Covid "panic button" that maintains the masses in a constant state of apprehension, fear, and submission. The controlled media channels their disinformation to the masses who uncritically accept as truth all claims of deaths caused by a pandemic.

THE CRITICAL ROLE OF 5G

Global surveillance cannot be universally achieved until 5G towers are constructed worldwide and a network of space surveillance satellites have been launched and are orbiting the earth. By the year 2030 Elon Musk's SpaceX corporation is expected to have 42,000 Starlink 5G citizen spy satellites in low orbit around the planet. By the first Quarter of 2021 there will be a sufficient number of satellites in service to trace and track vaccine injectees by homing in on vaccine-injected microdot ID. Approximately 60 satellites can be launched at a time; the menancing craft continuously circle the globe at an altitude of 210–710 miles above the planet's surface. (As compared to 22,000 miles for most orbiting spacecraft.)

Starlink satellites follow one after the other in orbit. SpaceX launches the satellites on its Falcon 9 rockets and expects to beam high-speed Internet to every location on Earth. But the true agenda is global surveillance and enabling the 5G Neuralink AI computer-human interface.

While Musk claims that filling the lower atmosphere with high technology frequency-generating devices is for providing Internet service at a more competitive cost than what is presently available, yet his timing perfectly coincides with the Globalist's Agenda urgent need to identify, trace and track everyone in the world. By transmitting and receiving one gigabit of data per second, his Starlink project is exactly what the globalist's needed and desperately wanted for enabling the seamless linkage between a globally present WIFi signal and Neuralink circuitry embedded in the brain of every human being. When any of the the fake pandemic vaccines are injected into the world's people, the hook up can then proceed to direct the mind, body and soul of the entire human race to obey and be controlled by the elites operating a technological control grid, and from which all those who are chipped by the vaccine can never hope to be free.

Presently, prior to the full implementation of Starlink, in Cuba and China there are reports among government diplomatic employees of ear pain, head pressure, dizziness, tinnitus, nausea, fatigue, anxiety, headaches, visual problems and cognitive difficulty such as memory loss and alteration of brain function. These are symptomologies of wireless pulsed radio and microwave frequencies emitted from 4G and 5G towers. Such RF effects are proven to be damaging to human health. The FCC is allowing the construction of 5G towers even though they are proven to be harmful to humans, animals, and the environment. Private property and indigenous land is not exempt from construction of the towers without consent.

Resistance at the community level has not stopped the spread of the growing number of ground-based 5G antennas, which will interface with Starlink orbiting satellite transmissions of the high-frequency radiation.

For over two decades the nanoparticulate Aluminum, Barium, and Strontium metallic components in Chemtrails have been inhaled and absorbed through the skin of everyone on the planet, and is consequently present in neural and somatic tissue to thus make people the equivalent of walking antennas for receiving 5G electromagnetic signals.

THE POTENTIAL FOR 5G TO CREATE VIRUSES IN VIVO

The following is an abstract from The Journal of Biological Regulators & Homeostatic Agents:

Coronavirus disease (COVID-19) is the main problem this year involving the entire world (1). This is an infectious disease caused by a newly-discovered coronavirus. This virus is a member of related viruses that cause diseases in mammals and birds. In humans, coronaviruses cause respiratory tract infections that can be mild, such as some cases of the common cold (among other possible causes, predominantly rhinoviruses), and others that can be lethal, such as SARS, MERS. COVID-19 is an enveloped virus with a positive-sense single-stranded RNA genome and a nucleocapsid of helical symmetry. The genome size of coronaviruses ranges from approximately 27 to 34 kilobases, the largest among known RNA viruses. To date, many scientists have tried to find a method to cure this disease, however, without success. COVID-19 may have effects on different types of cells. For example, it has been argued that this virus may have some effects on dermatologic cells. On the other hand, it has been known that some waves in 5G technology have direct effects on the skin cells. Thus, there are some similarities between effects of COVID-19 and waves in 5G technology. A new question arises regarding a relationship between 5G technology and COVID-19. The 5G technology is the fifth-generation mobile technology in which its frequency spectrum could be divided into millimeter waves, mid-band, and low-band. Low-Key words: **dermatologic antenna**; COVID-19; 5G technology; millimeter wave; DNA; inductor. In this research, we show that **5G millimeter waves could be absorbed by dermatologic cells acting like antennas,** transferred to other cells and play the main role in producing Coronaviruses in biological cells [Author's bold emphasis]. DNA is built from charged electrons and atoms and has an inductor-like structure. This structure could be divided into linear, toroid and round inductors. Inductors interact with external electromagnetic waves, move and produce some extra waves within the cells. The shapes of these waves are similar to shapes of hexagonal and pentagonal bases of their DNA source. These waves produce some holes in liquids within the nucleus. To fill these holes, some extra hexagonal and pentagonal bases are produced. These bases could join to each other and form virus-like structures such as Coronavirus. To produce these viruses within a cell, it is necessary that the wavelength of external waves be shorter than the size of the cell. Thus 5G millimeter waves could be good candidates for applying in constructing virus-like structures such as Coronaviruses (COVID-19) within cells. Corresponding researchers: Dr Massimo Fioranelli, Department of Nuclear, Sub-nuclear and Radiation Physics, Guglielmo Marconi University, Via Plinio 44-00193, Rome, Italy. 5G Technology and induction of coronavirus in skin cells M. Fioranelli 1, A. Sepehri1, M.G. Roccia1, M. Jafferany, O. Yu. Olisova, K.M. Lomonosov and T. Lotti1, Department of Nuclear, Sub-nuclear and Radiation Physics, G. Marconi University, Rome, Italy; Central Michigan Saginaw, Michigan, USA; Department of Dermatology and Venereology, I.M. Sechenov First Moscow State Medical University, Moscow, Russi.

SCIENTISTS WARN OF THE SERIOUS HEALTH EFFECTS OF 5G

In 2017, more than 180 scientists and doctors from 35 countries recommended a moratorium on the roll-out of the fifth generation, 5G, for telecommunication until potential hazards for human health and the environment have been fully investigated by scientists independent from industry. 5G substantially increases exposure to radiofrequency electromagnetic fields (RF-EMF) in addition to the 2G, 3G, 4G, Wi-Fi, etc. for telecommunications already in place. RF-EMF has been proven to be harmful for humans and the environment, and leads to massive increase of mandatory exposure to wireless radiation.

The following is from 5G Appeal 1

September 13, 2017

"We the undersigned, more than 180 scientists and doctors from 35 countries:

Wireless radiation 5G technology is effective only over short distance. It is poorly transmitted through solid material. Many new antennas will be required and full-scale implementation will result in antennas every 10 to 12 houses in urban areas, thus massively increasing mandatory exposure. With "the ever more extensive use of wireless technologies," nobody can avoid to be exposed. Because on top of the increased number of 5G-transmitters (even within housing, shops and in hospitals) according to estimates, "10 to 20 billion connections" (to refrigerators, washing machines, surveillance cameras, self-driving cars and buses, etc.) will be parts of the Internet of Things. All these together can cause a substantial increase in the total, long term RF-EMF exposure to all EU citizens. Harmful effects of RF-EMF exposure are already proven. More than 230 scientists from 41 countries have expressed their "serious concerns" regarding the ubiquitous and increasing exposure to EMF generated by electric and wireless devices already before the additional 5G roll-out. They refer to the fact that "numerous recent scientific publications have shown that EMF affects living organisms at levels well below most international and national guidelines". Effects include increased cancer risk, cellular stress, increase in harmful free radicals, genetic damages, structural and functional changes of the reproductive system, learning and memory deficits, neurological disorders, and negative impacts on general well-being in humans. Damage goes well beyond the human race, as there is growing evidence of harmful effects to both plants and animals."

After the scientists' appeal was written in 2015 additional research has convincingly confirmed serious health risks of RF-EMF fields from wireless technology. The world's largest study ($25 million) National Toxicology Program (NTP), shows a statistically significant increase in the incidence of brain and heart cancer in animals exposed to EMF below the ICNIRP (International Commission on Non-Ionizing Radiation Protection) guidelines followed by most countries. This is supported by results in human epidemiological studies on RF radiation and brain tumor risk. A large number of peer-reviewed scientific reports demonstrate harm to human health from EMFs. The International Agency for Research on Cancer (IARC), the cancer agency of the World Health Organization (WHO), in 2011 concluded that EMFs of frequencies 30 KHz–300 GHz are possibly carcinogenic to humans (Group 2B). However, new studies, like the NTP study mentioned above and several epidemiological investigations, including the latest studies on mobile phone use and brain cancer risks, confirm that RF-EMF radiation is carcinogenic to humans. The EUROPA EM-EMF Guideline 2016 states that "there is strong evidence that long-term exposure to certain EMFs is a risk factor for diseases such as certain cancers, Alzheimer's disease, and male infertility. Common EHS (electromagnetic hypersensitivity) symptoms include headaches, concentration difficulties, sleep problems, depression, lack of energy, fatigue, and flu-like symptoms."

The following is from 5G Appeal 2:

"An increasing part of the European population is affected by ill health symptoms that have for many years been linked to exposure to EMF and wireless radiation in the scientific literature. The International Scientific Declaration on EHS & multiple chemical sensitivity (MCS), Brussels 2015, declares that: 'In view of our present scientific knowledge, we thereby stress all national and international bodies and institutions . . . to recognize EHS and MCS as true medical conditions which acting as sentinel diseases may create a major public health concern in years to come worldwide i.e. in all the countries implementing unrestricted use of electromagnetic field-based wireless technologies and marketed chemical substances . . . Inaction is a cost to society and is not an option anymore . . . we unanimously acknowledge this serious hazard to public health . . . that major primary prevention measures are adopted and prioritized to face this worldwide pan-epidemic in perspective.'

"Per The Precautionary Principle (UNESCO), adopted by EU 2005: 'When human activities may lead to morally unacceptable harm that is scientifically plausible but uncertain, actions shall be taken to avoid or diminish that harm.' Resolution 1815 (Council of Europe, 2011): 'Take all reasonable measures to reduce exposure to electromagnetic fields, especially to radio frequencies from mobile phones, and particularly the exposure to children and young people who seem to be most at risk from head tumours . . . Assembly strongly recommends that the ALARA (as low as reasonably achievable) principle is applied, covering both the so-called thermal effects and the athermic [non-thermal] or biological effects of electromagnetic emissions or radiation' and to 'improve risk-assessment standards and quality.' The Nuremberg code (1949) applies to all experiments on humans, thus including the roll-out of 5G with new, higher RF-EMF exposure. All such experiments: "should be based on previous knowledge (e.g., an expectation derived from animal experiments) that justifies the experiment. No experiment should be conducted where there is an a priori reason to believe that death or disabling injury will occur; except, perhaps, in those experiments where the experimental physicians also serve as subjects.' (Nuremberg code pts 3–5). Already published scientific studies show that there is 'a priori reason to believe' in real health hazards. The European Environment Agency (EEA) is warning for 'Radiation risk from everyday devices' in spite of the radiation being below the WHO/ICNIRP standards. EEA also concludes: 'There are many examples of the failure to use the precautionary principle in the past, which have resulted in serious and often irreversible damage to health and environments . . . harmful exposures can be widespread before there is both 'convincing' evidence of harm from long-term exposures, and biological understanding [mechanism] of how that harm is caused.' 'Safety guidelines' protect industry—not health. The current ICNIRP safety guidelines are obsolete. All proofs of harm mentioned above arise although the radiation is below the ICNIRP safety guidelines. Therefore new safety standards are necessary. The reason for the misleading guidelines is that 'conflict of interest of ICNIRP members due to their relationships with telecommunications or electric companies undermine the impartiality that should govern the regulation of Public Exposure Standards for non-ionizing radiation. To evaluate cancer risks it is necessary to include scientists with competence in medicine, especially oncology. The current ICNIRP/WHO guidelines for EMF are based on the obsolete hypothesis that 'The critical effect of RF-EMF exposure relevant to human health and safety is heating of exposed tissue.' However, scientists have proven that many different kinds of illnesses and harms are caused without heating ('non-thermal effect') at radiation levels well below ICNIRP guidelines."

Deleterious genetic effects of 5G at the cellular and molecular level are well documented in the literature. When 5G is globally activated it will function in combination with Covid and all future biowarfare vaccine microchips. The RF and microwave signals from 5G cell towers and orbiting Starlink satellites are the information stream to the Neuralinked human brain. Pulsed 5G frequencies from these sources will cover every square inch of the planet with wireless radiation. When fully operational, there will be no where to escape from the invasive radiation assault upon the human mind and body.

NO WHERE TO RUN, NO WHERE TO HIDE

In municipalities all across America, the average citizen is video-recorded and photographed by government surveillance cameras more than 50 times every day. In the UK the rate is more than triple that figure, and in China it is 100 times these numbers. When

adding drone and satellite imaging, the surveillance capability for each country increases still further. With high-resolution cameras positioned at traffic intersections and inside and outside every commercial building, it has become nearly impossible to escape the ever watchful eye of the Orwellian "Big Brother" surveillance web. Facial recognition software instantaneously identifies anyone from a crowd; iris scans, fingerprint scans, and DNA profiling assures that one's identity can be database-verified. In addition to the globalist's cover story of fighting identity theft, terrorism, and illegal immigration, they now have the newly created rationale of a fake pandemic spread by an invisible nonexistent Corona Virus, and are thereby enabled to verify ID by scanned proof of vaccination.

The coming worldwide surveillance network encompasses much more than video documentation of your public whereabouts, and reaches into every aspect of your private affairs. High-tech snoops are watching you in your home, at work, at play, and even in the most innocuous situations where you may feel safe from unwelcome intrusions. For instance, the television and Internet affords easy access for prying into your life, whether through 2-way TV screen optics or NSA/FBI government data-mining operations such as Facebook, Twitter, Instagram; or simply by accessing Google or other search engines, where your computer ID, IP address, and location are available for prying eyes to see. Your personal information, preferences, views and opinions are stored in a dossier data file. Anytime you log onto the Internet a government agency such as the NSA, BATF, or Office of Homeland Security knows about it. Google logs every webpage you visit, every word search, website, video, or book you view; every email message you send or receive is noted and recorded. Artificial Intelligence robots instantly offer suggestions on what may appeal to your interests. Spy software in your iphone and computer listen to your every word and can deduce what you're thinking. In essence, your thoughts are no longer your private property; privacy no longer exists; you are transparent and therefore vunerable. This should provide any rational person the motivation to disconnect from the electronic cage.

The globalist mentality would like you not to be concerned that your every word, deed, and even your thoughts are public knowledge, for, why should you be anxious if you have done nothing illegal? But that is a false and misleading premise utilized by the power elites to wrest more control from the citizenry. Upon considering that police have been granted the right to enter private residences and conduct warrantless searches (HR6666) and to arrest and quarantine healthy peaceful citizens suspected of harboring a nonexistent virus, your privacy and personal communications should be of the utmost importance for your safety and well-being.

A total surveillance control grid will have been achieved at the point when nearly everyone on the planet has been vaccine-microchipped for enslavement to the Globalist's Agenda. Imagine a world of forgotten individuality, of great masses of brainwashed mind-controlled people too freightened to even so much as whisper in protest of the overbearing tyranny. It will be a world of micro-chipped robot-like creatures without a mind of their own, completely dependent upon Lucifer's government for supplying (and denying) their basic needs. It will be a world of lost souls, no hope, no future. That day is not far off, fast approaching, and is presently less than a decade away. The future of mankind has already been determined, and only the individual has the capacity to make a choice to change their course and alter their immediate destiny. There are two possible decisions to make—either for Jesus Christ, or for the Globalist's Agenda. Failure to make a conscious choice for the former will default to being controlled by the latter.

All who stand against government tyranny, the fake pandemic, submission to bioweaponized vaccines, will one day find them self in a similar situation. Prepare now for that future eventuality (ref. Appendix A).

In a Police State society the body is held captive but the mind can yet be free. Wicked men may put chains on human hands and feet, but they can never arrest and imprison your soul—unless you allow them. If you grant them permission to inject a vaccine microchip into your body, or by any other means submit to Satan's 666 number or the number of his name, you have given his government people permission to not only destroy your body, but more importantly, you will have allowed them to take captive the spirit of your soul. Upon receipt of a fake pandemic vaccine, you and your children may soon die, or will cease from being human, and the future will be dark and without hope. It will be a time of dependency upon government, extreme compliance, abject obedience, constant terror, loss of freedom and dignity.

You must realize that what is in jeopardy is far more than your physical and psychological health. It is your eternal soul. The stakes are indeed that high.

"HAPPY SHOT." After being injected with Covid vaccine biowarfare components at a FEMA-supported mass vaccination site, Janice M. of North
Carolina exclaimed, "I'm so happy I got my shot!" Billions of uninformed
media-brainwashed people will likewise voluntarily choose death over life,
unaware of the consequences.

CHAPTER 6

TRANSHUMANISM, VR, NEURALINK, AND THE FOURTH INDUSTRIAL REVOLUTION

"Isn't the only hope for the planet that the industrialized nations collapse? Isn't it our responsibility to bring that about?"
—Maurice Strong, former Under Secretary-general of the UN, Chairman of the Earth Summit, as he delivered an official statement

Modern technology is presently advancing at such a rapid pace that computer efficiency is doubling every 18 months. Over the span of just two decades computational speed grew at an exponential rate and computers achieved a certain threshold when instantaneous retrival of all the world's pool of knowledge by means of the WiFi Internet was made possible. Soon, AI quantum computers and man will become integrated, and independent Free Will shall be merely a vague memory from the distant past.

For the first time in history total control of the entire world population is possible through instantaneous wireless transmission. As a consequence of ultra-high speed nanotechnology via 4G and 5G, there was born the world of interactive Virtual Reality, a technology that is a weaponized form of television. Like TV, a VR captive audience can be brainwashed, mind-controlled, and programmed to uncritically accept the political, social, and religious ideology of the globalist's Luciferian indoctrinations.

"Any Reality. Anywhere. Anytime," could become the slogan of the elite world controllers desperate to force their will upon the unsuspecting masses. A VR "alien invasion" or the "Second Coming of Jesus Christ" are technological illusions that could be globally transmitted to serve their diabolical madness. A computer-generated Virtual World is a realm where anything can be real, and nothing is real. It is the ultimate great deception of the human spirit, a major advancement of the Agenda to create a synthetic reality that can be utilized for human control and as a political tool where truth and falsehood are interchangeable, and where there is no moral difference between good and evil, right and wrong.

The implications of nanotechnology are far-reaching and clearly portends the future of mankind. By instantaneous global communication the elites have at their command a ready means to manipulate and deceive the mind of the entire human race. From nanorobots to microchip-directed DNA spliced into the human genome for altering the genetic code, the fake pandemic Covid vaccination agenda is an integral and essential component for bringing about a political slave state. As the race toward the oblivion of mankind marches onward, increasingly more human Free Will shall be sacrificed to the globalists. If God were to allow it to proceed to conclusion there eventually would be no distinction between human and robot, and an artificial "android species" would emerge, one without autonomy or a soul. *Matthew 24:22: And except those days should be shortened, there should no flesh be saved: but for the elect's sake those days shall be shortened.* Fortunately, the integration of man and machine will never take place on a large scale because, just as during the time of Noah—when human-demon hybrids resulted from the spiritual genetic mixing of fallen angels with humans (Genesis 6:4)—God intervened to destroy the quasi-human race, and, except for Noah's family of eight, Satan's contamination of the human gene pool was wiped out in a worldwide flood.

The book, The Fourth Industrial Revolution, was written by the Founder and Chairman of the World Economic Forum, Klaus Schwab, an understudy of Adolph Hitler's eugenics and mind-control of the masses. His vision is world Fascism, the state protecting the interests of the wealthy elite. He termed his evolution of man-machines "The Great Reset," where all of humankind has become linked to Artificial Intelligence (AI) via the 5G (and 6G) Neuralink satellite control grid. With the pretense of enhancing human mechanical and cognitive capability (i.e. according to the expectations of the global psychopaths) by the year 2025, one-third of the jobs now performed by humans will be replaced by software, robots, and smart machines. By the year 2030, programmable babies will be the standard for populating the last generation prior to the prophesied return of Jesus Christ. Schwab intends to accomplish his twisted goals via *nanotech-bioweaponized vaccines*.

Internet Article: **Globalist Klaus Schwab: "As Long As Not Everybody Is Vaccinated, Nobody Will Be Safe"**

Speaking at this year's Davos Agenda, World Economic Forum (WEF) Founder and Chairman Klaus Schwab declared "nobody will be safe" until "everybody is vaccinated" with the COVID-19 immunization.

The man behind "The Great Reset" plans on using the pandemic to usher in a new era where the global elite retain total control over humanity.

One reason Schwab and his ilk would like to vaccinate as many humans as possible is to implement a Big Brother-style surveillance system equipped with the latest spy technology.

Schwab's WEF writes, "Faced with deep recession, governments around the world are considering the use of immunity passports to allow a degree of normality to return."

Klaus Schwab: "As long as not everybody is vaccinated, nobody will be safe." pic.twitter.com/EtfyZFCqyl—Disclose.tv ? (@disclosetv) January 29, 2021

Libertarian icon Ron Paul warns against such a change, saying:

"The great reset will dramatically expand the surveillance state via real-time tracking. It will also mandate that people receive digital certificates in order to travel and even technology implanted in their bodies to monitor them."

"The system of tracking and monitoring could be used to silence those expressing 'dangerous' political views, such as that the great reset violates our God-given rights to life, liberty, and the pursuit of happiness," Paul added.

NEURALINK TRANSHUMANISM

AI robotics and quantum computers will continue to increase in speed and efficiency to produce a series of human-like robots that can simulate rational compelling dialogue on any subject accessed from 5G and 6G global WiFi network wireless communication. The rapid development of robotics has advanced to where the "ghost in the machine" looks and acts human; the only aspect lacking is a moral conscious.

Recently, AI robots were made to self-program without the assistance of man, and that was the turning point at which microchip technology began to be applied to the electronic circuitry of the human brain. Implantation of nano-biochips—part human DNA and part nonhuman silicon nanobytes—will create a cyborg chimera that commands superintelligence capable of competing with the rapid development of AI machines. The disturbing implications of this represent the endpoint of mankind.

Elon Musk, clearly being directed by indwelling demons, plays a major role in creating the link between man and machine.

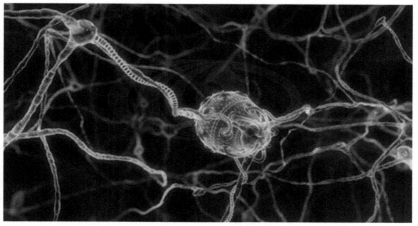

Micrograph of nerve cell: nanobots replacing neurons.

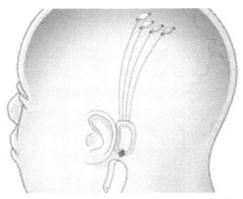

Neuralink connectivity to the global 5G WiFi Starlink network.

As the End Year 2051 approaches, and accelerating from the year 2030 onward, humanized robots will become everywhere present—teaching in the schools, ruling in government offices; occupying positions in commerce, entertainment, sports; and in the home, where robo-mothers and robo-fathers replace the absent parents or provide social companionship and sexual gratification for the lonely man or woman. Virtual emotions will become the standard in a microchipped genetically-modified 5G and 6G Neural-linked global society. It will be a world populous that has lost natural affection, loves and obeys the virtual government, despises the Christian ethic, worships the Antichrist, and rejects Jesus Christ as the only ligitimate authority. There will be a steady progression in the loss of characteristics which define humanity, until the image of man becomes fully degraded into the 666 Beast system image of Satan. When that point is reached it will be the Globalist's Agenda End Game, and it shall be a time that coincides with the return of Jesus Christ, which will be the "Ultimate Great Reset."

FUTURE TIMELINE DETAIL OF EVENTS

Near-Term

Spring 2020: Globalist's reign of terror begins with fake news media reports of a nonexistent pandemic. Beta-testing of citizenry forced to wear ineffectual masks, social distancing, urgency of a vaccine "savior."

January 2021: Roll-out of the Covid vaccine in America. 300 million doses of C–19 vaccine soon available. Early stages of select groups (e.g. elderly over 75: eugenics) injected with vaccine containing pathogens, toxic elements, programable microchip and CrispR gene-splicing capability. Escalating disinformation, announcement of viral "Variants" requiring more vaccines (binary trigger) and more restrictions on human rights and freedom. Ongoing reports of deaths from Corona Virus are fabricated disinformation. (Exponential death rate is caused by the Covid *vaccine*, not the faked virus.)

June 2021: General population vaccinations. Widespread distribution of the injectable *Covid bioweapon*. Elon Musk's SpaceX 5G Starlink Satellites globally activated as an Internet Service Provider (a pretense for global citizen surveillance and Neuralinkage of the world population).

Fall (Sept–Oct) 2021: Mandatory and forced vaccines. Refusal to be injected will result in arrest, fine, jail, vaccine injection, FEMA Death Camp. Citizen protests and violent resistance expected among a cognizant small minority. There is going to be a civil protest to the mandatory vaccinations when Satan's government people demand that everyone submit to a Covid death shot and show a scannable ID vaccine validation as proof of having been vaccinated (luminescent tattoo on index finger, or forehead, or hand) in order to enter public and commercial establishments or conduct any kind of business transaction, including buying food, employment, school, banking, etc. (October 2021: "Compliant" auto license plates to allow entry into Federal buildings or TSA flights without supplying additional documentation. Black star on plates to signify the mark of Lucifer's satanic government.)

The year 2021, and the subsequent period to 2030 and beyond, will incrementally escalate protests of the fake pandemic tyranny when the invasive tattoo is upgraded and infused into the deep skin layers on the back of the right hand or forehead. At that point there will be a severe backlash and violent revolt among the few True Christians throughout the world. Deaths at the hands of the police and FEMA incarceration will subsequently follow.

From an Internet Article posted on February 9, 2021: *"Multiple people shot at Minnesota clinic; one detained."* The news report failed to mention the reason or motivation for the shooting, omitting that it was a protest against the Covid vaccine being administered at the hospital. This fact was conveniently left out of the report because it would create awareness among the sheeple and trigger more violent protests, shootings, loss of life to those blinded to the vaccine deception and to those front line "useful idiots" (doctors, nurses, and other healthcare workers) who mindlessly demand submission to the Covid death shot. Shooting incidents will increase in frequency as the government demands for mandatory vaccines escalate. The focus will then shift to gun confiscation and removal of self-defense weaponry from the citizenry.

The Luciferian globalists will never stop until they vaccinate everyone on the planet, or kill off the remainder in the process. As Satan's servants, they are harvesting souls. All those who were destined to capitualate to their demands will follow them to their demise in the Lake of Fire. Revelation 13:10: *He that leadeth into captivity shall go into captivity: he that killeth with the sword must be killed with the sword. Here is the patience and the faith of the saints.*

Intermediate-Term

2022: Top in the U.S. financial markets. Covid business shutdowns and quarantines; business and bank failures to soon follow.

2022–2025: Crash of the U.S. and world economies; severe devaluation of the Dollar currency, replaced by a digital global noncurrency accessible by scanning device; luminescent tattoo microchip embedded in human body (index finger/right hand/forehead).

2025: Cashless world economy (Covid viral transmission: pseudo-justification for cashless currency).

2025–2028: Planned SPARS fake Pandemic; never-ending series of ongoing pandemics and viral-specific bioweapon vaccines.

2025–2030: Stages of global dictatorship: formal dissoluton of U.S. and all the world's nation-states; emergence of a global government with a single dictator as World President—the Antichrist.

(Most likely candidates at this time are Barack Obama, Bill Gates, Jared Kushner, Elon Musk.)

2029: Potential for an asteroid impact on Earth; unfolding of other Revelation prophesies signaling God's Judgment upon mankind. Revelation 8:8–12: *And the second angel sounded, and as it were a great mountain burning with fire was cast into the sea: and the third part of the sea became blood; And the third part of the creatures which were in the sea, and had life, died; and the third part of the ships were destroyed. And the third angel sounded, and there fell a great star from heaven, burning as it were a lamp, and it fell upon the third part of the rivers, and upon the fountains of waters; And the name of the star is called Wormwood: and the third part of the waters became wormwood; and many men died of the waters, because they were made bitter. And the fourth angel sounded, and the third part of the sun was smitten, and the third part of the moon, and the third part of the stars; so as the third part of them was darkened, and the day shone not for a third part of it, and the night likewise.*

Long-Term

2030: Worldwide transition to digital identification and cashless monetary noncurrency is complete. Mark of the Beast Luciferic tattoo mandatory. The "New Normal" is fully accepted by the mind-controlled masses as a replacement social reality. The globalist's New World Order is finally realized.

2030–2050: Human-computer interface: Transhumanism, alteration of human genetic code (genome) and loss of human identity resulting from chromosome contamination with vaccine gene-spliced nonhuman DNA; further population reduction by "Variant" vaccinations, mass sterilization through the Covid and Spars vaccines. Globalist's attain total control over the world's population via Starlink surveillance, gene insertions and deletions, programmable microchip vaccines under the false flag pretense of an ongoing series of worldwide fake pandemics. Multiple doses of vaccines will serve as a mechanism to activate previous vaccines that trigger a severe physiological reaction culminating in death. Vaccine resisters will be cut off from commerce and sent to FEMA Death Camps; Christian persecution, beheadings (Rev. 20:4).

2051: Return of Jesus Christ. End of First Phase of the 3-dimensional Earth reality. Great White Throne Judgment. Phase Two is the 1000 year higher-dimensional Millenial Kingdom New Jerusalem, with simultaneous conclusion of 3-dimensional Earth reality. The subsequent final Phase Three will be the destruction of the earth and local space, replaced by supra-dimensional new Earth and new Heaven. *And I saw a great white throne, and him that sat on it, from whose face the earth and the heaven fled away; and there was found no place for them. And I saw the dead, small and great, stand before God; and the books were opened: and another book was opened, which is the book of life: and the dead were judged out of those things which were written in the books, according to their works. And the sea gave up the dead which were in it; and death and hell delivered up the dead which were in them: and they were judged every man according to their works. And death and hell were cast into the lake of fire. This is the second death. And whosoever was not found written in the book of life was cast into the lake of fire. . .And I saw a new heaven and a new earth: for the first heaven and the first earth were passed away; and there was no more sea. And I John saw the holy city, new Jerusalem, coming down from God out of heaven, prepared as a bride adorned for her husband. And I heard a great voice out of heaven saying, Behold, the tabernacle of God is with men, and he will dwell with them, and they shall be his people, and God himself shall be with them, and be their God.* (Revelation 20:11–15; 21:1–3).

SATANIC HOLIDAYS:
KEY DATES FOR GLOBALIST'S AGENDA

- December 21, 2020: Winter Solstice: roll out of the first Covid–19 Vaccines. The Winter Solstice is when the European Union (EU) officially kicked off its Covid–19 vaccination campaign days after approving the BioNTech/Pfizer Corona Virus vaccine.

- Hollywood film, "Songbird," planned to come out at the end of 2021. It is pre-emptive programming for conditioning the mind-controlled world masses to a never ending C-19 fake pandemic script: C-21, C-22, C-23 . . . .

- March 21, 2021: Vernal Eqinox: pre-planned second wave of Corona Virus "Outbreak"(fake C–19 "Variant").

- June 21, 2021: Summer Solstice: accelerated phase of vaccine global distribution. Pre-planned third wave of Variant Covid "outbreak."

- From December of 2020 to June of 2021 (from the Winter Solstice to Summer Solstice), Covid vaccines will first be distributed to select groups (medical staff, elderly), then to the general public. (By June 2021: sufficient Space X Starlink Satellites will be in orbit for 5G/microchip-global surveillance.)

- September 22, 2021: Autumn Eqinox: *Mandatory* C–19 vaccines. Expected citizen revolt, rioting, clashes with Satan's government people. Dissidents killed or jailed and sent to FEMA camps.

Additional Dates:

- 2025: Amazon One Contactless Pay at U.S. Super Bowl. Palm Pay system. No cash accepted; wave hand over a scanning device. ("Palm Pay" readers are presently being deployed in Walmart stores and will soon be universal throughout all retail and other means of commerce. The device will then transition from reading the biometric underside of the hand, to decoding the Revelation 13 Mark of the Beast luciferase quantum dot tattoo vaccine Validation Certificate embedded on the top side of the hand.)

- 2025–2028: SPARS pre-planned Pandemic (CoroVax). A presently existing detailed plan with specific future dates for implementation, including death statistics, variant vaccines, lockdown quarantines, closings of business and public services, etc.

- 2029: Apophis Asteroid expected to collide with Earth.

- 2030: Enactment of Agenda 2030. Full implementation of Neuralink, 5/6G (666G) Starlink, cell towers, CrispR gene-splicing, upgraded weaponized Covid/SPARS/etc., Variants, more vaccine injections.

CHAPTER 7

THE DESTINY OF THE GLOBALIST ELITES AND THEIR NEW WORLD ORDER

And the kings of the earth, and the great men, and the rich men, and the chief captains, and the mighty men, and every bondman, and every free man, hid themselves in the dens and in the rocks of the mountains; And said to the mountains and rocks, Fall on us, and hide us from the face of him that sitteth on the throne, and from the wrath of the Lamb: For the great day of his wrath is come; and who shall be able to stand?
—Revelation 6:15–17

The rich men of the world, the globalist elites, will be hiding in the mountains, living underground in subterranean cities hollowed out beneath the earth by machines like those of Elon Musks' Boring Company. They shall be desperate to escape the wrath of God, but cannot, and will be forced to experience the full impact of His vengeful fury. In their anguish and distress they will cry out for help, but there will be no one to save them; their master, Satan, father of lies, will have long since abandoned them to die a prolonged and painful death.

The saga of humankind began in the Garden of Eden, a pristine tropical paradise where organic food grew out of the ground, the air was clean, the water pure. But, there was something lurking in the shadows, and the globalist's ancestor—the shape-shifting snake— stalked the first humans to their death. Man subsequently bore the consequences of a world immersed in evil and ruled by the Serpent's seed—the generational crime familes of the world, the globalists. As the progeny of the Great Deceiver, they are representative of the most wicked men and women in history; for thousands of years their names have been associated with notoriety, and their deeds will follow them into eternity. These, the offspring of Satan, are the rich men of the world who despise God and his Word, and who sought to rid themselves of his righteous commands. All their life, through the agency of their controlling demon spirits, they were conveyed instructions on plotting and scheming to exterminate mankind. They planned well, but not well enough, for, in the end they were proven to be fools who merely thought themselves wise.

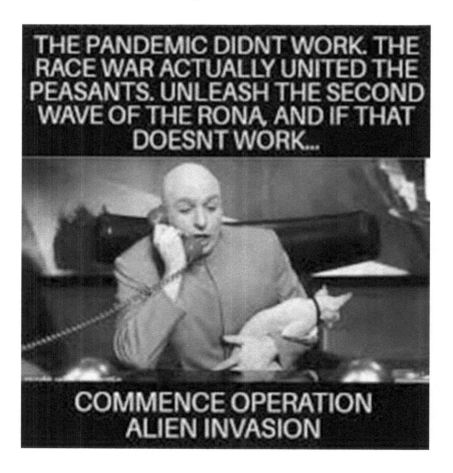

The presumed masters of the destiny of mankind never ask permission, they just take whatever they want. To them, people are cattle, commodities to be exploited for their own benefit. True psychopaths lacking empathy or a conscious, their heart has been severed from their soul; they feel none of the pain which they cause the rest of humanity. Their only interest is in themselves, their money, their power, and their service to Satan, which is largely an unwitting desire to be God. Since at least the 1950's they have poisoned the food supply through genetic engineering and toxic chemical additives; they poisoned the municipal drinking water supply with Fluoride and Lithium to tranquillize the citizenry; they poisoned the ground water with Fracking horozontal oil drilling, they poisoned the air with Chemtrails and electromagnetic radiation that damages human, animal and plant chromosomes; and through toxic government they poisoned the human race over whom they presume to rule. They own and control the media so that people all over the world never have the opportunity to hear the truth, only lies from their scripted fake news censors. Remaining behind the scenes, they control all the world's governments and transformed the U.S.A into a corporation, an entity run by the Illuminati supra-state Federal Reserve private centralized banking cartel. Their crimes against humanity comprise a long list of transgressions against God and his creation. Their master, Satan, rules in the schools, churches, and homes. Everything is corrupted by their unseen hand, and children are their primary target. Hollywood, TV, the music industry, mainstream news, Google Internet, are all part of their media purview; no aspect of modern life is left untouched. They used computer technology to create a seamless web of lies and deceit which the unSaved masses of the world are unable to perceive. They fabricated a pandemic to bring down the world's economy and enslave everyone in their invisible Vaccine/Neuralink/Starlink control grid. In the end, they corrupted and destroyed everything that God had created perfect. For all this, and much more, the judgment wrath of God is soon coming to redress the evil which they have done.

The assured fate of the global elites is quite simply the Lake of Fire. It is a certainty which none of them shall escape, for, every one who did evil works will not only die a horrific death when exiting this life, but also an even more terrifying and painful fate when dying a second time in the never-ending Lake of Fire. The payment for their unrepentant wickedness is eternal, and they cannot circumvent the fast approaching destiny which God has prepared for them. They were used for his own purposes, as a test to see who among mankind would follow them. Nearly everyone rejected the Almighty Creator of the universe, Jesus Christ, and obeyed Satan's government people, all the way to the burning pit of everlasting torment.

The globalist's New World Order—The Great Reset, Fourth Industrial Revolution—will never become established upon planet earth; it will dissolve into nothing upon the return of the KING of kings and LORD of lords (Revelation 19:16). Their plan will be extinguished before it gains sufficient momentum to change the image of God into the image of Satan. After all their lies, deceits, murders and destruction, their warped vision will come to nought, and all that will remain is the eternal Judgment of an angry God. When standing before the Great White Throne, the Bill Gates' of the world shall beg for mercy, but the Eternal Judge, Jesus Christ, will grant them no mercy. No amount of money, no promises, no lies, no deceit, no deal, will change His mind: https://www.youtube.com/watch?v=958G-zzqgWnw. "I never did nothing to nobody." (Frank Lopez to Tony Montana: Scarface.)

The real test on planet Earth is to obey God and keep his Commandments, not to obey wicked men intent on evil designs. Scripture advises in Acts 5:29: *We ought to obey God rather than men.* In the Great Earth Experiment very few people believed God, and even fewer obeyed him. Consequently, a large portion of humanity is rejected by God because of their unbelief and unrepentent heart.

The death of mankind is a planned destruction of souls, for not everyone will follow the narrow way that leads to salvation. There is a very small number of individuals who go on to a greater glory than what this material life has to offer. All the rest are consumed, like human carcasses harvested by the elites to feed their insatiable hunger for death and destruction. Only 1 in 2000 rejected lies and believed and obeyed the Commandments of God (Ecclesiastes 7:28).

The Lake of Fire is a substantively real place; it is not some religious concept or fantasy, but is a higher-dimensional realm located in hyperspace, and referred to in the Bible as "Outer Darkness," a vast, burning, smoldering plain of boiling sulfur and brimstone which appears as a seething pool that stretches to the horizons. It is a realm of darkness and timelessness, inhabited by the most savage and sadistic demons (Genesis 6:4). The heat, the stench of burning rotting flesh is unbearable; multitudes of millions gasping for air, howling in pain; large grotesque spirit beings tormenting and torturing all those who did evil upon the earth. This is not a scene from a Spielberg film; it is reality.

For the Illuminati globalists, their future is dark and without any hope. They sinned to the greatest degree possible, and it was a most egregious offense to the God of Truth and Life. They sought to transform humanity into a sterile robotized machine, a souless mechanized nanobot computer without a Free Will to choose good over evil. They destroyed the earth, they destroyed mankind; and they did it at the command of their leader, Satan, the fallen chief angel, aka Lucifer.

In the end the children of Satan pay an infinite price for what they did while in the flesh. They are beyond salvation, for where there is no repentance, there is no forgiveness. The Bill Gates genre of mankind have absolutely no future in the most bleak scenario possible: no escape from the darkness and suffering, agony and torture. For an eternity of time they will reside in a realm of no light, hope, or mercy; only torment and pain to match the degree of their crimes against God and his precious creation.

The globalists calculated, they planned, they executed well, but in the end they failed, and death is the only destiny they will ever obtain. All that they had done to afflict the world's people—the pain and suffering, the torture and torment; all the tears, all the disappointments and all the deaths, will come back upon their heads and continuously haunt them for time without end. They shall wail throughout an infinity of regrets for all their evil, and the only memory they shall retain in a place of perpetual darkness is the pain and suffering, torture and torment, tears, disappointments and deaths they caused others. It will be all they would ever know—for eternity.

So, take heart, dear reader, the King of Heaven is a righteous Judge, and everyone will receive their just recompense at the throne of God Jesus Christ. With each passing day that eventuality becomes an inevitable certainty, and only a brief span of time temporarily delays it. The cross you must bear at the hands of the Luciferian globalists and all those who obey and follow them, will be as nothing compared to what they will be forced to experience. And, whereas, for you it will soon end; for them and for all those who submit to the Covid/Spars vaccines, there will never be a cessation of the wrathful Judgment of a righteous God: *And the smoke of their torment ascendeth up for ever and ever: and they have no rest day nor night, who worship the beast and his image, and whosoever receiveth the mark of his name* (Revelation 14:11).

The elites believed with all their black hearts that their Agenda was the purpose for their lives, yet they were deceived, and it was only God testing them to prove their unworthiness for a future in Paradise. They lied, they cheated, they stole, they murdered, they insulted God every day of their wicked existence; they entirely missed the point of life. Those whom they persecuted, tortured and murdered, are translated to a higher-dimensional world of tranquillity, harmony, peace, beauty and serenity that surpasses anyone's ability to even imagine. Their pain and suffering was the price they paid for defending the truth; their reward is to eternally reside among the epitome of truth itself, Jesus Christ. The wicked are judged and condemned; the righteous are vindicated, forgiven, and shown mercy. Cosmic justice, in the end, shall prevail.

SALVATION BY THE NUMBERS

While the Luciferian globalists are busy depopulating planet Earth, God is also culling mankind. His eyes search the globe for that one who will obey him and be his faithful servant. According to Ecclesiastes 7:28: *Which yet my soul seeketh, but I find not: one man among a thousand have I found; but a woman among all those have I not found.* By direct correlation, this translates into 1 in 2000 that are Saved into the Kingdom of Heaven. All the rest end up in Hell. *Narrow is the way, which leadeth unto life, and few there be that find it* (Matthew 7:14). Contrary to what is taught in the 501(c)3 government "churches," the number of condemned souls is higher than anyone presumes.

As long as the Sheeple remain passive and acquience to the insanity of today—wearing a mask, not forming groups, not rising up against tyranny and exposing evil, obeying criminal government, submitting to a weaponized vaccine; and, instead of shouting "No!" they sheepishly whisper "Baaaaaaa"—they will continue to be sheared.

Presently, the U.S. population is 330 million

330 million/2000 = 164,000 Saved people in America at this time

164,000/51 States = 3215 per State (includes DC)

3215/10 large cities per State = 322 per city (populations range from 5,000 to 8 million)

Cities and areas with the following populations will average the below number of Saved individuals (population divided by 2000) at any given time:

Population	Number of Saved people
10,000	5
100,000	50
200,000	100
500,000	250
1,000,000	500
etc.	

These numbers vary according to situation. In some locations there will be a higher proportion of Saved people. For example, families may show a greater incidence of individuals who accepted Jesus as their Lord and Savior, than is seen among those who are associated with government. *Turn, O backsliding children, saith the Lord; for I am married unto you: and I will take you one of a city, and two of a family, and I will bring you to Zion* (Jeremiah 3:14). Proportionally, there are likely to be more who are Saved in random segments of the population at large than is found in organized religion and in buildings which are proclaimed as being "The Church."

What is happening now in human history is strictly a *spiritual issue*. Before our very eyes we are witnessing the separation of the sheep from the goats (Mathew 25:31–46), the wheat from the tares (Matthew 13:24–30). For this author, the only surprise is just *how many* people are going to hell. He never thought it would be 1999 out of every 2000, and instead just assumed it would be something like 9 out of 10, or even 2 out of 3. But, according to Scripture (Eccles 7:28) there are far more whose destiny is the eternal Lake of Fire. Until the occurrence of the fake pandemic, and upon witnessing people's submission to satanic government mandates—obeying Satan, disobeying God (Matthew 6:24); and while observing the indications of their *lost status*: the wearing of a mask, social distancing, submitting to the Mark of the Beast vaccine, believing the Covid lie—the author never realized the vast numbers that actually translate to hell. On an average day of going about your routine, you are not likely to encounter even one person who is Saved and destined for Heaven.

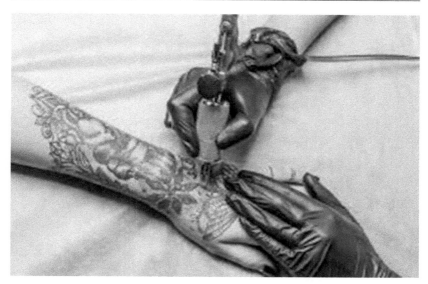

The globalist's-promoted paradigm for psychologically acclimating the world culture to an acceptance of marking the human body with an indelible subdermal tattoo has conditioned people to submit to a Luciferase tattoo marking them with the damning fake pandemic Corona Virus Mark of the Beast. Those so marked are subject to the eternal wrath of God (Revelation 13:16,17;14:9–11). Tattoos are a form of self-mutilation. Leviticus 19:28: *Ye shall not make any cuttings in your flesh for the dead, nor print any marks upon you: I am the LORD.*

A CALL TO ACTION:
WHAT YOU CAN DO

And five of you shall chase an hundred, and an hundred of you shall put ten thousand to flight: and your enemies shall fall before you by the sword.   —Leviticus 26:8

The author believes that one person can make a substantial difference in the world. This is because they can reach out to other people and expand their influence, which goes exponential at a steadily increasing rate. Why do you suppose all the Internet social medias have banned any posts that reveal the Covid lie? It is because through those media the globalist's can lose the battle for the destruction of humanity; their plan can fail if enough people "catch on" to what they are doing. Currently there are a significant number of individuals who will refuse the mandatory vaccine, but what they don't realize is that Satan's government people will simply deny them access to participate in commerce by forcing them to prove they have been vaccinated—digital ID fingerprint scan—and without which no food can be purchased, no buying or selling of any kind can be transacted. Play it out in your mind and you will see that is a doomsday scenario. When people get hungry they will do anything, even at the expense of the loss of their soul. Presently, very few have the information to make an informed decision regarding vaccinations (ref. Ch 4: CDC false reporting of Covid deaths and vaccine injuries), and those with the knowledge and wisdom to know not to submit to Satan's sorcery are being censored. Therefore, we must continue to inform and educate at all levels of one's sphere of influence. By promoting the truth you will be among a very small minority in your community. Soon it will be nearly impossible to circulate truthful Covid information, therefore, work while there is yet light (ref. John 9:4). Be prepared for the police to confront and arrest anyone who speaks against the Covid farce, or who is randomly scanned and found not to be vaccinated. Stephen King could not have devised a more diabolical plot.

ROUND-UP READY

Envision a scenario where a small group of people suddenly remove their face masks and let them drop to the ground. Then, eyes fixed straight ahead—their faces stern as flint, and arms at their sides— with fists tightly clenched, they start walking.

They walk until meeting others who likewise are not wearing masks. Soon, more maskless small groups are formed, and which combine to create larger groups of well-informed committed individuals who understand the issues. Awakened from a deadly slumber, they comprehend what they must do. With a sense of purpose the growing assemblage moves steadily forward as they accumulate numbers, a veritable army, steadfast, set on a course to expose lies told by the controlled media and believed by a cognitively-paralyzed public who faithfully parrot the Covid deceit. They march on, gathering strength, fully realizing that there is no pandemic and everyone in the world is not at risk of endangering their health. They stopped believing the globalist's pernicious lies, and now, armed with the truth, they stand in defiance against the many who are yet in denial and wear a mask; those who strive to silence them with arrest, jail, and even legally-sanctioned murder.

Their numbers continue to grow while they boldly speak out against a carefully-crafted plot to destroy mankind with nothing more than the pretense of something to be feared. People gather around, most shout obcenities and threaten to attack them, others are silent, and a few join them as they continue marching onward.

There is a list of names which the gathering storm has compiled, and it consists of the names of those who plotted to overthrow God and his creation. One day the massive crowd of avantgarde protestors arrive in an area of great wealth and oppulence, where the driving force behind the global charade resides in luxury and safety from the consequences of the evil which they have perpetrated. It is where the Bill Gates' reside, and where the Mark Zukerburgs live, the Elon Musks, the Ray Kurzells, and all those thousands of other insiders who thought they were insulated and protected from the repercussions of their wicked deeds. But, they are not invincible, and one by one, each on the list is rounded up, drug out of his house, and summarily executed.

The end of the Covid reign of terror exactly coincides with the extermination of the demonized individuals who took it upon themselves to direct human destiny into a realm from which there was no going back. But, this scenario does not end there . . . it continues on into infinity.

REFUGE FOR THE SAINTS DURING THE GREAT TRIBULATION

When they deny you service to buy food, just realize that hunger is a temporary condition, and if you have fasted before you will realize there comes a point where you are no longer hungry. Also, you have about 30 days to wait on God to provide food, and if he does not, then you will soon be in a place where you can eat or not eat, and it is all organic (grows on trees). The Scripture (Revelation 12:6) tells of a place of refuge which God will provide during that time. The author knows of no such location, and it is either figurative symbolic language or somewhere like the Amazon jungle. Of course, the only reason why God would wish for any of his people to remain alive during this present Tribulation time is to speak the truth and spread it far and wide, not to hide and do nothing. Therefore, all those who are truly of God will be evangelists, bolding speaking the truth while teaching and preaching the testimony of the Bible. The true people of God must persevere until the end, for there is no "Pre-Tribulation Rapture" (Matthew 24:29–31). Those who believe otherwise give evidence of not being Saved.

By the year 2030, a detailed personal dossier of everyone on the planet will have been compiled and stored in a permanent data base for instantaneous retrival from globally-linked supercomputers throughout the world, such as "The Beast"—a tetrabyte control processing unit located in Brusels Belgium—that can store trillions of bytes of information on every person extant on the globe. The total surveillance grid will be inescapable at that point, and evading government scrutiny will become increasingly more difficult for those who refuse to be vaccinated or marked by any of various means described in this book, and who are not otherwise "in the system." For the few with the spiritual foresight not to form an allegiance with the tyrannical Beast by silently "Opting Out," there will be fewer places and ways to hide. Bank accounts, insurance, utility bills, tax records, medical and educational documents; auto license, title and registration; Internet service provider, credit card purchases, etc., can no longer be associated with your identity. If you want to get the criminal government out of your life, you must be entirely "off the grid." Yet, even a dilligent expungement of your presence from public records will one day find you in a face-to-face confrontation with the police during a routine traffic stop, highway vaccine check point, or while relaxing at a public park, where you are reported by a TV/Internet-programmed vaccinated/microchipped citizen of the New World Order who swore allegiance to the Luciferian globalists, and who thought you looked "suspicious" (i.e. Satan's demons told him you were there and who you are). Counsel to the wise: Take immediate steps to extricate yourself from the present and coming future oppression. In as much as possible, remove from civilization and completely disconnect from the surveillence grid. Needless to say at this juncture, do not get vaccinated or submit to any form of government identificaion, digital ID, tattoo, injected microchip, etc. *A prudent man foreseeth the evil, and hideth himself: but the simple pass on, and are punished* (Prv 22:3). You must hide yourself, yet, whenever and however possible, proclaim the truth to a truth-denying world. Stand up and speak out. The worst that you can do is to remain silent.

The only rational course of action to be taken in the face of tyranny is to say "No." At each incremental stage where government demands are being made, access is denied. No permission is ever granted; no edict is ever obeyed, or even so much as acknowledged. Anything originating from a satanic illegitimate government, or from any governmental representative, is to be ignored, then scorned, publicly ridiculed, and treated as a preverse attempt at despotism. This attitude is the heart of someone who loves the truth, who hates evil—in all its varied forms—and who steadfastly refuses to compromise. Such an individual realizes that even a slight concession in acknowledging illegitimate authority is a step backward and will subsequently require still more ground to be lost to the avaricious demands of the world controllers. Civil war abolishionist, Fredrick Douglass, understood this well when he stated: "Find out what people will submit to, and you will have the exact amount of tyranny that will be imposed upon them, until resisted with words, or blows, or both. The limits of tyrants are prescribed by the tolerance of those whom them oppress."

The Bible differentiates between murder and killing. The act of killing is not prohibited by God's Word; murder is prohibited and is defined as the shedding of innocent blood (Psalm 10:8). The blood of God's enemies is not innocent, therefore, the killing of God's enemies is not a transgression of the Laws of God. *We ought to obey God rather than men* (Acts 5:29). For a true Christian, obeying God's Commandments is a virtue, not a vice (Deut 7:1,2).

In the UK there were some who burned 5G towers, realizing its link with the Covid fake pandemic. Action taken by citizen activists has not proven to be an effective long-range strategy to stop this facet of the globalist's vaccine/5G/ Starlink operation.

Through human programming, mind-control, and fear, the few control the many. But the few are extremely fearful of the many, and that is why their plan for the total subjugation and control of all of humanity has been kept secret for so long. Transparency can severely compromise the globalist's plans, so those plans must remain hidden from view by compartmentalization in order that even the buracracy itself does not perceive the big picture of what is occurring all around them. Exposure of the Globalist's Agenda puts them at risk for a violent backlash from a public that has been made aware of the globalist's diabolical intentions. The global elites are fearful that, armed with truthful information, the U.S. citizenry may rise up and deploy the over 300 million guns in a civil war to defend themselves from tyrannical invasion of their lives. This is the primary reason for the social distancing, home quarantines and lock-downs—it is an effective means to prevent a potential uprising by keeping people sequestered and unable to interlink with others that could result in formulating an effective course of action. This is why the world controllers must maintain a constant flow of traumatizing disinformation and escalating falsehoods of a pandemic. They maintain control though lies and deceit.

The "Republican party" is pro-guns; the "Democrat Party" is anti-guns. (There is no "2-party" system in America. It is merely the Hegelian Dialectic, controlled opposition intended to pacify the people to think they have a choice, when in fact, they do not.) Biden's Administration will be a coup d'etat of the peoples of America when he neutralizes the threat of guns which could be used to thawart the Globalist's Agenda. One way the globalists will do this is by confiscating registered guns and by prohibiting the sale of ammunition.

Staged shootings are pre-planned by the CIA and other departments within the U.S. government, such as BATF and Homeland Security, to elicit a fear response from a fearful citizenry demanding gun control. Once again, it is the Hegelian Dialect of Problem (mass public shootings)—Reaction (citizens fearing for their lives)—Solution (legislation to confiscate guns). The shooters are MK-Ultra Trauma-base programmed by their Handlers to respond on cue with rampage killing of random people. Many of them are suffering from vaccine injury and are on psychotropic drugs. The controllers will continue with this tactic until they achieve their desired outcome of a disarmed America. Yet, they will encounter difficulty when attempting to completely remove guns from the hands of those who realize the gun grab is only a pretense for total takeover. The current and future generation has been indoctrinated in the government public schools to believe that guns are "bad" and need to be "outlawed." The globalists are waiting for the present generation to die out, and with them, the truth about "gun control."

In Leveticus 26:8 God ordains a course of action for dealing with tyrants: *And five of you shall chase an hundred, and an hundred of you shall put ten thousand to flight: and your enemies shall fall before you by the sword.* This key Scripture is a guide to direct action against those of a lesser god, and who have determined to destroy the image of a holy and righteous God. Maintaining the groups in small sizes—5 familiar friends—prevents government infiltration and the possibility of defection. Once several such groups are created they can then interlink to expand into a much larger group of 100 or more informed and committed individuals that God will enable to accomplish much more than any of the smaller groups could achieve by acting independently.

Failure to take the initiative in rising up against tyranny will inevitably result in the loss of freedom, loss of life, and possible loss of one's soul (forced vaccine). Organizing like-minded individuals for the purpose of devising a workable strategy to rise up against despotism is God-approved advice. Hebrews 10:25: *Not forsaking the assembling of ourselves together, as the manner of some is; but exhorting one another: and so much the more, as ye see the day approaching.* It is not "unpatriotic" to make a stand for the truth; it is cowardice, unrighteous, and revolting in the eyes of God to not oppose, expose, and fight against tyranny. Jeremiah 48:10: . . . *cursed be he that keepeth back his sword from blood.*

Out-numbered 100 to 1, criminal government fears the people of America armed with 325 million guns. The most effective means the globalists have to prevent an overthrow by an informed citizenry is their controlled media spewing forth a constant stream of lies and disinformation. Neutered males, a morally bankrupt society, and a brainwashed mind-controlled chemically-pacified public insures the success of their global Agenda.

NEUTERED MALES

A testosterone deficiency in men results in passivity, apathy, complacency, and an unwillingness to stand up in defense of the truth. Males who lack a sufficient quantity of this hormone circulating in their blood tend to exhibit a low level of energy, sedentary lifestyle, under achievement, reduced physical and cognitive activity; they are unconcerned and disinterested about today's totalitarian world events. A reduced level of blood serum testosterone is associated with sterility and a lowered sperm count. The reason for these symptomologies can be manifold but are almost always the result of environmental factors such as consuming weaponized food/beverages, and vaccines.

Common sources of testosterone-binding agents that render a man passive and less virile are: Monosodium glutamate, Aspartame, High Fructose Corn Syrup, fluoridated tap water, fluoridated bottled water fed to infants, BPA plastic food and drink containers. Some known dietary causes of low levels of testosterone and sterility in men are: Soy products, trans-fats, hormone-treated meats and eggs, pesticides, refined sugar, processed packaged foods and beverages, fluoride from various sources (e.g. tap water, toothpaste, dentist), and genetically modified food products. Infant and childhood biowarfare vaccines are by far the most effective means to decrease masculine behavior in the male population throughout the world.

Today, especially in America, males have been castrated by the culture. In word and deed they bear no resemblance to the men of yesterday, those who rose up and fought against the tyranny of their day—the colonists of 1776; the idealists of WWI and WWII. On the scale of "Maleness," as a group, men have presently shifted toward the feminine side of the gender spectrum. They no longer stand up and fight, but instead remain seated and silent, with not even so much as a whimper of protest. They will put on their mask (and be certain it covers their nose), not stand or sit too closely to those around them in public, and will shun any talk of vaccine "Conspiracy Theory." They are brainwashed, media-controlled, compliant obedient slaves of the Luciferian authority which dictates their behavior. In other words, they are not men.

As infants and children, they were vaccinated. Although there is also the issue of their lack of moral fiber, yet that deficiency is overshadowed by vaccine-induced biological changes which have occurred in their brains to alter them from being an "intact" male to becoming a genetically-castrated quasi-male.

Early childhood vaccines were designed by the globalists to alter gender. Today's incidence of homosexual men and women is in direct proportion to the administration of vaccines. The gay Agenda is an aspect of the Globalist's Agenda, and is a consequence of neuro-logical changes which occurred during infancy and young childhood, as well as from the destruction of the nuclear family, where the male dominate role was subsumed by the single mother (e.g. 80 percent of Afro-Americans were raised without a present father). This familial pattern has profound long-term implications in terms of establishing male identity.

Even the most outwardly virile is complicit by their lack of public response to the fake pandemic. Large body, but small heart, they will not rise up and shout from the roof tops: "We've got to stop this! Now!" It is indeed a rare individual who will risk his comfort and safety by making a stand for the truth. Although some may be "big and strong," and perhaps even "work out at the gym" to attain bulging muscles, yet none will outwardly challenge those who seek to enslave and destroy them. Neither will they put forth the time and effort to study the issues and discover what the globalist's are doing and planning to do. They will not take action until it is too late, and will remain passive, silent, and feminine. Such a person is not a biological male; he is a self-absorbed coward and a disgrace to man-hood. In nearly every instance, *that* is what exists today, especially in America.

The modern man is actually a quasi-male. He is not "fully intact," having been castrated and neutered by vaccines and a modern Lucif-erian society. Masculine values are foreign to him; he only knows to keep his mouth shut and to submit. The globalists realize this, for indeed, it was they who created him. His testosterone production significantly reduced by food and beverage doping, his genetics changed by infant and early childhood vaccines, he was never an intact male in the usual sense, and as an adult, is rated somewhere between a boy and a girl—not fully a man, a chimera; part female, part male. The farthest thing from his/her mind is to make a public stand for the truth. *That* he will never do. He simply does not possess the male equipment. (Satanists are known to castrate their young male children and feed them female hormones to produce a hybrid male/female.)

At the other end of the gender spectrum is the dominate female. These, commonly known as "Dykes" or "Jezebels," are increasingly encountered in today's lockdown society, and have assumed male behavioral characteristics in response to the globalist's orders to maintain the Sheeple in a constant state of fear and submission. One of the ways they accomplish this is by controlling others, and especially men, by a demand to wear a mask while in a public setting. All social propriety vanishes when the alpha female commands mask-wearing compliance; never is that stated as a request, but always as an order. Failure to obey immediately defaults to "Calling the Police." Rational argument is of no avail when attempting to reason with a testosteroned-woman who revels in her ability to neutralize a much more powerful and physically capable opponent. With hands figuratively tied behind his back and several police 40 caliber handguns pointed directly at him, jail is in his immediate future . . . because he refused to display a sign of submission and allegiance to the globalist's master, Satan. As the atypical valiant defender of truth is led away in handcuffs to an awaiting police cruiser, the masculine female gloats over having attained yet another victory in a male-dominated society ordained by a male God. However, what she does not realize is that her man-domineering actions are in direct disobedience to God, as it is written in 1 Timothy 2:12: *But I suffer not a woman to teach, nor to usurp authority over the man, but to be in silence.* For her disregard for the law of God in usurping authority over a man, she will be sternly judged. Males are made in the image and likeness of God, and in challenging a man's God-ordained status in having dominion over a woman, she has challenged God Himself. For that, she will pay an eternal price.

Blood in the streets. This is what is required to stop criminal government.

This is the reality of obedience to evil rulership and failure to stand up, speak out, and defend the truth from all powers, foreign and domestic.

The loss of freedom occurs in stages, it is incremental. With each concesssion the individual loses more of their liberty and Free Will, and the usurper gains more power to control. It is a gradual weakening process until one's personhood degrades into a symbiotic relationship with the ravenous Beast system. The loss of individuality can be a subtle erosion of values by compromise, absorption into a larger entity, like osmosis of a pure liquid into a slowly swirling dark pool of sewage. The individual is absorbed by a sinister malevolent force that feeds off the life blood of others. The loss of personhood may also occur all at once, as whenever saying "Yes" to yet another government decree. At each conceeded demand the probability of subsequent acquience increases still further, until the mind is no longer one's own, but has become the property of the parasitic state. The time soon arrives when the once free and independent man gazes up from the ground, a jackboot stomped on his bloodied neck, and in a pathetic patronizing plea, whispers, "I love you Big Brother." Obeying the demands of a criminal institution—an unrighteous authority under the purview of Satan—involves the most severe of consequences: irrevokable, incontrovertible, permanent, with no hope, no life, no future, for all of eternity. It is indeed the Lake of Fire, and once that decision is reached, there is no going back.

YOU HAVE ONLY 2 CHOICES: DEFEND YOURSELF, OR DIE

You must be brutally honest, and ask, "How much am I willing to risk to protect my life, my health, and the lives and health of my children and future posterity? What does this mean to me in terms of what I will do to stand up against evil, the globalist usurpers, the servants of a lesser god? And what will it take to repel, prevent, and utterly stop them from tresspassing upon my personhood and those whom I love and have a responsibility to defend? What do I need in order to accomplish that objective? How can I obtain it? Where is it available?' The author recommends Lasers; they are silent, fast acting, easily concealed, require no training to operate, are nonlethal (you

World: Hobbyist injures self with 1 watt blue laser

19 Dec 2011 - Damgines: Foch evident evidence ; Eye effect or injury ; Updated: xliv

A laser hobbyist was injured by a 1 watt 445 nanometer (blue) laser on December 6 2011. The injury required unspecified surgery, possibly removal of intraocular blood via needle. Two days after the surgery, the hobbyist reported a blurry dark circle in his central vision. His doctor told him he would always have a small off-center blind spot, and that his brain would "auto-correct" to fill in the spot.

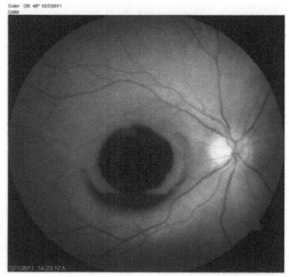

laserpointersafety.com

do not need to kill anyone), and are effective for instantaneously burning the occular retina and rendering an assailant unable to see. If they cannot see you, they cannot grab you. This will afford you a chance to escape to safety.

Make a pocket-sized hand-held Laser yourself, or consult with someone in the Physics Department at your local University. Hand-held Lasers of greater than 5mW are illegal. While the author does not recommend doing anything illegal—when dealing with an unConstitutional illegitimate Illuminati globalist entity planning to vaccinate, microchip, gene-splice, trace and track, hook you up to a global Hive Mind Neuralink, and send you to a FEMA Camp for torture and extermination—preservation of one's life and the life of one's spouse and children takes precedence over totalitarian rule by an oligarchy of genocidal psychopaths. Blue light Lasers (not red or green) are the most effective, and are available on the Internet for purchase (approx \$10–\$50). Overseas manufacturers advertize their Lasers as 5mW, but are actually much higher output: 1.5W (1500x), which is sufficient to get the job done and is capable of disabling any New World Order quasi-human instantaneously. (The diode and lithium batteries can be upgraded to produce 5000x.) Even 1–3mW Laser pointers can cause blindness. Be certain to always wear high-end Laser safety glasses when activating the Laser. Do not use welding glasses, shields, or the glasses which may be included with the Laser kit.

Internet resources will likely soon disappear once this information becomes general knowledge, so hurry and purchase in quantity (50–100 to give to family and friends) for having a ready stockpile of small, hand-held, concealable, self-defense weaponry that is likely one day to prevent you from being taken to Camp FEMA. To avail yourself of this last remaining loophole to stand against tyranny, check these Youtube links and others like them for more details: https://www.youtube.com/watch?v= W6FbUiiwutQ, https://www.youtube.com/watch?v=DMVWW –bmKwQ&feature=emb_rel_end

An intelligent rational individual thinks ahead; he or she does not wait until the inevitable moment occurs. Plans are made, a strategy is formulated far in advance of the actual event. During the present time when there is yet some degree of safety and freedom to choose (as of January 2021), an astute person will conceive and plan a detailed course of action. You may not be able to preserve your life in the face of all the many and varied obstacles which are soon coming; you may not survive at all, and you may die at the hands of snarling mad dogs come to claim you as their property. But you owe it to yourself, and even more to your family and loved ones, to have made preparations to resist and evade, to the best of your ability, any and all attempts to lay hands on you and take you where you do not wish to go.

THIS:

Physical death might cause pain, or it might not. Pain will leave you shortly and your spirit will lift off your motionless body and drift away—hopefully upward.

OR THIS:

The globalist's are serious. So should you be. Play rough and you might get hurt; wait for a frothing mad government drone to grab you, and you will surely die. There exists a vast power disparity between you and criminal government. THIS levels the playing field. Use it only when there is no other option. https://www.youtube.com/watch?v=DMVWW −bmKwQ&feature=emb_rel_end, https://www.youtube.com/watch?v=W6FbUiiwutQ

No matter the consequences, you absolutely must make a stand for the truth. To remain silent is to be complicit, and, much more, you have denied Jesus Christ by not speaking out to warn others with the truth for all to hear. Ezekiel 33:6: *But if the watchman see the sword come, and blow not the trumpet, and the people be not warned; if the sword come, and take any person from among them, he is taken away in his iniquity; but his blood will I require at the watchman's hand.* That will be the greatest indictment against you on the final Day of Judgment, when the King of kings asks you, as you stand before his Great and Imposing Throne, "Why didn't you occuppy 'til I come?" (Luke 19:13). What will you answer? And when he says, "I advised you to hide yourself (Prv 22:3). Why didn't you?" What will you reply? Will you also remain speechless when he says, "I told you to go out into all the world and preach the gospel (Mark 16:15). You didn't do it. Why?" What will be your response when he says, "I advised you to sell your garment and buy a sword (Luke 22:36) . . . but you didn't. Why not?" And he will surely ask you why you buried your talent and did not invest it to yield much increase for His Kingdom (Matthew 25:14–30). How will you be able to justify yourself when your Creator is gazing directly at you, and the portal to Hell is opening just behind you? Be aware that God is not a respector of persons, and he does not care in the slightest who you think you are, or what others think of you. Perhaps you have deceived yourself into believing you are "a good person," one who is bound for heaven. Maybe your friends, associates, and Pastor have told you that. But God does not judge on the basis of opinions, wishful thinking or appearances; he judges the heart, the true intentions; what you do, what you say, and what you fail to do and say. He hates evil, he hates evildoers, and he hates those who tolerate them (Revelation 2:2). *I know thy works, and thy labour, and thy patience, and how thou canst not bear them which are evil: and thou hast tried them which say they are apostles, and are not, and hast found them liars.* In tolerating evil, in allowing it to proliferate by remaining silent and not speaking out in condemnation against it, you yourself become evil, and God hates you for that. In Revelation 21:8 there is a list of those who are cast into the Lake of Fire. The first to go are the cowards, the fearful: *But the fearful, and unbelieving, and the abominable, and murderers, and whoremongers, and sorcerers, and idolaters, and all liars, shall have their part in the lake which burneth with fire and brimstone: which is the second death.*

To enter the Kingdom of Heaven your actions must match your good intentions. Otherwise, you will be among the hypocrites whom God sternly condemns throughout the Bible. If you are merely a Christian in name only, then your profession of faith is a fraud and you are an impostor. You will not be able to stand in the Judgment if there is no fire in your heart for the righteousness of God. If you can allow wickedness to prevail over goodness, how can you claim to know a holy and perfectly righteous God? How can you stand by and watch the evil ones destroy His image and likeness? You do not have to tell this author your reply, because he already knows what is in the heart of someone who does not love God. The great warriors of Biblical times all understood that what they were doing in confronting the enemies of God was actually defending the truth from being overtaken by lies. The King Davids, the Joshuas, the Gideons, the Sampsons, the Moses' and Aarons, and all those who made a stand against the evil of their time, first and foremost loved God above everything else, even their own life. And the Prophets and Apostles of old did not waiver, but stood in the face of evil while boldly, confidently, calling evil, evil; and good, good. They were courageous—even though some of them may have been afraid— yet, courage is not the absence of fear, but rather, it is action taken despite overwhelming fear. Some of them lost their lives fighting for the truth; all of them were immediately translated into an infinity of indescribable peace, comfort, and beauty. They were willing to experience a cessation of physical existence because they knew what the stakes were, and to them death was merely a small token to pay for the glory of the King and an eternal future in Paradise.

The time is fast approaching when you will have to make a decision. Prepare your heart now, while you still can. Devise plans, and perhaps God will bless them and grant you the victory, if not in this world, then most assuredly, in the next. Go forth from this time forward by the power of God Almighty and do not fear the enemy, but know instead that the enemy fears you, because the power that is within you is infinitely greater than the power of those who seek your life (1 John 4:4). Always maintain an eternal perspective and remember who you are in Jesus Christ.

Isaiah 41:9-13, 17,18: *Thou whom I have taken from the ends of the earth, and called thee from the chief men thereof, and said unto thee, Thou art my servant; I have chosen thee, and not cast thee away. Fear thou not; for I am with thee: be not dismayed; for I am thy God: I will strengthen thee; yea, I will help thee; yea, I will uphold thee with the right hand of my righteousness. Behold, all they that were incensed against thee shall be ashamed and confounded: they shall be as nothing; and they that strive with thee shall perish. Thou shalt seek them, and shalt not find them, even them that contended with thee: they that war against thee shall be as nothing, and as a thing of nought. For I the Lord thy God will hold thy right hand, saying unto thee, Fear not; I will help thee. . . . When the poor and needy seek water, and there is none, and their tongue faileth for thirst, I the Lord will hear them, I the God of Israel will not forsake them. I will open rivers in high places, and fountains in the midst of the valleys: I will make the wilderness a pool of water, and the dry land springs of water.*

Everything will be brilliant light, and you will experience a deep sense of peace. Someone will be standing right in front of you. It will be Jesus. Most everyone thinks of him in terms of being merely a concept or an ideal, not a real person; they cannot envision that the person actually exists. When you met him, you will say, "Are you the one in the Bible?" He will say "Yes." And then, the Judgment.

SHEMITAH, JUBILEE CYCLES, AND THE END YEAR 2051

In Jewish theology, a Shemitah is a 7 year cycle, and a Jubilee consists of 49 years. There exists several key relationships between these calendar time measurements and the past and future history of mankind. The following is an illustration of how these passages of time relate to the End Year 2051.

In God's Word, the Bible, the number 7 signifies completion or perfection.

Shemitah 7 year period x 7 = 49 years = 1 Jubilee year

From the time the nation of Israel crossed the Jordan River, after a 40 year exile in the Sinai desert, by the year 2051, there will have been 70 Jubilee cycles.

49 x 70 = 3430 years

3430 years x 5 days per 360 day year (Jewish calendar) = 17,150 days

17,150/ 360 days= 47.6 years

3430 years + 47.6 years = 3478 years

2050 – 3478 = 1428 BC = the time of the nation of Israel crossing the Jordan River to enter the Promised Land

3478/a 49 year Jubilee cycle = 70 Jubilee cycles = the number for completion

September 10, 1952: Signing of War Crimes Agreement between Israel and Germany. (God reconciles his judgment wrath upon the nation of Israel.)

September 11, 2001: Destruction of NYC World Trade Towers. (The commencement of God's judgment upon the Gentile world—America and the inhabitants of planet Earth. Destruction of NYC Trade Towers was a prelude to the 2020 start of global government, and was a declaration of captivity for the world's people.)

69th Jubilee Cycle: September 10, 1952—September 11, 2001

September 10, 2050: The 49th year of Jubilee prior to the return of Jesus Christ in the year 2051. (In the year 2012, God showed this author that the year 2051 would be the year of his return.) 2051 is the fifthieth year of the seventieth 49 year Jubilee cycle.

70th Jubilee Cycle: September 11, 2001—September 10, 2050

Allowing for additional days of the Jewish calendar, seventy Jubilee cycles **will end in the year 2051.**

Therefore, in the year 2051, Jesus Christ will return to Earth, and at a time of maximum chaos created by the Globalist's Agenda. All the issues described in this volume will have reached the full expression of evil upon mankind.

Those who are unschooled in Scriptures, or who otherwise lack spiritual discernment to comprehend the meaning of God's Word, will quote Matthew 24:36: *But of that day and hour knoweth no man, no, not the angels of heaven, but my Father only.* The author makes no claim of advance knowledge regarding the day or hour for the return of Jesus Christ. Only the year has been revealed to him by God.

Currently, at the time of this writing, according to the Bible (Revelation 13:16,17), the people of the world are about to be vaccine-microchipped under the pretense of a fake pandemic. After more than 2000 years of history, the time has finally arrived for the fulfillment of this prophesy. June 21, 2021, Summer Solstice, will be the key date to watch, since it will coincide with the mass distribution of the vaccine bioweapon to the spiritually dead people eagerly waiting in line to be jabbed with a death shot that will likely be the cause of their premature demise, and that will condemn their soul to eternal torment. The next date to watch is September 22, 2021, Autumn Equinox. This is an even more critical date because it is when compliance with the Covid farce will be mandatory. At that time millions of people in America, and perhaps a billlion globally, are going to be on the run from government terrorism, and also from persecution by rabid masses of the vaccinated deceived citizenry who will stalk, assault, and report them for "vaccine noncompliance." The *autumn of 2021* is when the Illuminati globalist human-demon hybrids are going to open the flood gates of hell.

SAFEGUARDING YOUR HEALTH FROM DESTRUCTION BY THE MEDICAL CRIME CARTEL

*Bless the L*ORD*, O my soul, and forget not all his benefits: Who forgiveth all thine iniquities; who healeth all thy diseases; Who redeemeth thy life from destruction; who crowneth thee with lovingkindness and tender mercies; Who satisfieth thy mouth with good things; so that thy youth is renewed like the eagle's.* —Psalm 103:2-5

The Medical Crime Cartel, also known as the Medical Criminal Fraternity (MCF) ref. *Genesis 1:29 Diet, The Criminal Fraternity,* is an organized network of medical health-related groups, organizations, and individuals all working toward the same goal of maintaining the general population in a state of compromised ill health. By the use of their pharmaceutical drug trade this global hierarchy strives for control over all those who submit to their drug sorceries. (The word "Pharmacy" is derived from the Greek "Pharmakeia" which transliterates to "Sorcery"—i.e. Witchcraft.) Availability of alternative treatments and cures are discouraged by the MCF and even prohibited.

Positioned at the top of the command and control pyramid is the Rockefeller crime family. Since the time of the family's patriarch, John Davison Rockefeller in the late 1800's, the medical establishment has been directed by a system of covert rules, regulations and medical practices which are designed to kill off and weaken by illness and disease the global population. This depopulation agenda is promoted under various guises by the European Rothschild-controlled media as beneficial and health-engendering, yet, the long-term results are a projected reduction in the number of people upon the earth to a bare minimum (95% kill rate), and a rendering of the remainder cognitively unfit to function without a dependency upon the MCF's pharmaceutical drug trade. Their targeted depopulation agendas implement the strategic use of weaponized vaccines, weaponized food, weaponized water, weaponized breathed atmosphere, and weaponized electromagnetic frequencies. Each of these facets are detrimental to human health and contribute to a decline in the physical and cognitive integrity of the global population.

What the founding father of the Rockefeller dynasty realized early on was that he could create organizations which operate under the pretense of health care, when in fact the true objective of those organizations was, and continues to be, the degradation of public health and a reduction in human numbers. His Sloan-Kettering Institute and American Cancer Society are two examples of health care facilities ostensibly engaged in researching ways to cure cancer, but, in truth, exist solely to discover or create new ways to proliferate and spread more virulent kinds of cancer among the general population. The reason why cancer has remained a seemingly intractable medical problem for so long is because a cure would significantly diminish profits from the Medical Crime Cartel's stranglehold on public health. (There are many ways to cure cancer using alternative approaches to organized medicine; these means are censored, and the promoters are either exiled or murdered. Ninety-five percent of cancer treatment patients die from the chemotherapy and radiation treatment, not from cancer.)

Statistically, 50 percent of the U.S. population is afflicted with some form of cancer, and over one third are plagued by Diabetes. (The other two thirds are likely in the early stages of Type II Diabetes.) The third leading cause of death in America is Upper Respiratory Disease, which has a direct causal link to Chemtrails, vaccines, and airborne environmental pollutants, including laboratory bioengineered viruses such as Mers, Sars, and the various Corona Virus Influenzas. (Covid is merely another species of Influenza.) It can be proven that these leading causes of death and disability are directly attributed to the MCF agendas to depopulate the planet. Their own documents—e.g. Agenda 21, Agenda 2030, Report from Iron Mountain, Protocols of Zion, and their Project for the New American Century (PNAC), state the central role of global depopulation by means of creating stealth diseases and "incurable" afflictions that can only be treated with their ineffectual expensive pharmaceutical drugs.

An invisible enemy "phantom pandemic" like "Corona Virus" does not require any basis in reality for the dumbed-down public to accept it as "truth." All that is required is the media-instilled perception of an imagined threat to public health. Nearly every disease prevalent in modern societies is by design and purposively induced by the elite generational crime families as part of a long-range plan to both generate massive pharmaceutical drug profits, and at the same time exterminate from the planet large numbers of "excess people." The Agendas to depopulate extend into every aspect of modern society, from the food that is consumed, to the air that is breathed. No intrusion into the human body has been overlooked: food, water, air, bioengineered stealth diseases, vaccine injections, the electromagnetic cage, 5G radiation, and contact with the deadly Medical Crime Cartel—all major pathways for sabotaging and destroying physical and psychological health.

While professional medical criminals may appear to be well-meaning and sincere (or are just convincing liars), they are extremely dangerous to be around, not only because of their profound degree of health-related ignorance, but also due to their position within the MCF hierarchy, which confers upon them a mystique as an unquestioned expert in matters of health; a definitive authority which may neither be questioned nor refuted. Doctors, as representatives of this criminal organization, function as middlemen in the pharmaceutical drug trade when dispensing pharmakeia prescriptions and vaccine "death shots" to their uninformed patients. A significant part of a doctor's occupation is the administration of drug prescriptions to the general public; and vaccines to infants, children, and adults. Their occupation is a crime against humanity, since those same vaccines were never designed or intended to cure, but only to maim and kill.

The MCF cannot operate in a society of well-informed people that are made aware of the dangers of remaining ignorant in today's genocidal world of witchdoctor medicine. The organized medical crime syndicate enlists it's media disinformation campaign in an effort to maintain the world populous in a state of irrationality and blind trust upon a health care system built on a solid foundation of lies and deceit. Naive individuals watch a TV commercial promoting a pharmaceutical drug to treat (not cure) their present distress, never realizing that the long list of cited adverse health effects are a certain clue to the ineffectiveness and detrimental health consequences of the drug or treatment therapy. Without access to the truth, a media-programmed public is divorced from reality and is easy prey for those who profit from the MCF's devious and diabolical concoctions. Ultimately, all those many who believe a lie will suffer the consequences in terms of diminished physical and cognitive health, premature aging, induced pharmakeia sorcery maladies, and vaccine injuries—all provided by the Medical Crime Cartel at no extra charge.

WHY DOCTORS CANNOT CURE YOU

It is actually quite easy to be healthy and totally free of illness and disease. You don't need doctors or to observe the latest fad diet; no need for some arcane sage advice about a new discovery promising to make you feel better, look younger, and live longer. And you do not have to join a health club to engage in strenuous exercises or boring group classes that merely leaves you more exhausted, while accomplishing nothing in regard to eliminating diseases acquired by dietary practices, vaccines, resistant obesity from ingesting foods and beverages laced with MSG, Aspartame, and factors that create Acquired immunodeficiency—all of which no doctor knows how to recognize, diagnose, or effectively treat. Contrary to conventional wisdom, attaining a state of perfect health has nothing to do with the development of bulging skeletal muscles; it does not require a popularized diet or esoteric formulations with a long list of vitamins, minerals, and "superfoods" to somehow make you healthier. There exists no relationship between a disease-free state of perfect health and visits to a doctor's office. One should never appeal to conventional medicine, which is a racketeering syndicate with no useful knowledge, wisdom, or motivation to restore and maintain you in a state of vibrant health.

If you follow the counsel of God as written in the 1611 King James Bible, he promises that you will be renewed to a time prior to when the manifold schemes of wicked men were conceived. If you take seriously God's Word, your health will be fully recovered, and it will be maintained throughout the duration of your life—for as long as you observe the counsel of the Wise. His promise is this: *Behold, I make all things new* (Revelation 21:5).

God does not lie. Whatever he says in his Word, he creates. *In the beginning God created the heaven and the earth. . . . And God said, Let there be light: and there was light* (Genesis 1:1,3).

DOCTORS ARE DOOMED

There is a myth that exists in most moden societies which presumes that a doctor is in possession of extraordinary curative powers that defy the inferior limited understanding of the common lay person. This gross misconception is reinforced by the media and the culture to such a degree that good health is often considered synonymous with a toxic dependency upon doctors and the mad medicine they support. In reality, nothing could be further from the truth.

The first nail in the doctor's coffin is the erroneous notion of "The Good Doctor." Surely, if they were somehow able to magically transform a person to a state of glowing health, they could likewise achieve the same result for themselves. But, alas, they cannot, and the reality is that, on average, doctors live 10 fewer years than the general population. Doctors cannot cure, and the best they can do is medicate symptomologies with pharmakeia drugs in an ineffectual effort to obscure and exacerbate the underlying cause of physical distress. Failing that, they will simply cut "something" out, radiate, or chemically inject with lethal toxins until the patient either runs out of medical insurance coverage, or dies. Afterall, the entire medical health care fraud is not about being healthy, it is about making money. It certainly is not about making people well.

The second nail in the doctor's burial casket is the fact that he or she knows little or nothing about the fundamental role which diet plays in promoting good health. While atttending medical school there was one 50 minute lecture regarding basic nutrition, and which anyone could learn in 5 minutes by searching Online for FDA Minimum Daily Requirements establishing nutrient levels in the human body. That 50 minutes is all the formal training a doctor has received about the single most important factor determining a disease-free healthy state of being. The remainder of a doctor's training is largely occuppied with studying biochemical interactions of the body's physiology with pharmaceutical prescription drugs. (This is an Illuminati protocol. The global elites write the medical text books, fund the "scientific" research, and determine the content and emphasis of a doctor's curricula.) Essentially, the well-meaning, but naive, medical student became an unwitting pawn as a middleman in a global drug sting enterprise with an agenda to maintain the populous in a state of ill health and diminished cognitive function. Seldom does the brainwashed intern come to the realization that eugenics, genocide, and depopulation will be the final result of their many years of laborious study. It is indeed a pathetic and devious occupation to assume control over people's health, when, in fact, one is diligently striving to undermine it.

The third nail in the doctor's grave box is a forced relationship with the American Medical Association (AMA), which insures that he or she will never deviate from the globalist's prescribed depopulation Agenda. Without question, or even so much as venturing to voice an opinion, the "Good" Doctor will follow orders that have come down from the top of the Satanic Pyramid of Power (ref. The Globalist's Agenda). It is instructive to stand back and ponder the duplicity and lack of moral conscious that is required of the typical doctor who remains complicit by his willful ignorance and silence. Millions of infants, innocent little children, and the elderly have suffered at the hands of the doctor, nurse, or other health care practitioner who raised a hypodermic needle to inject a toxic brew of Autism-inducing ingredients directly into the blood stream of the trusting recipient. The distressed child wails in shrieks of pain while the parents look on and stupidly smile their approval, and the doctor and hospital receive a "kick back" monetary reward for each administered death shot. This unconscionable act is criminal, and the implications for the child's future potential is tantamount to premediated First Degree Murder. Legal consequences should follow, but do not.

MD's are visual proof that people rise to the level of their incompetence. Doctors do not, and cannot, cure illness and disease; they *cause* illness and disease. In ancient Rome they were considered to be a pernicious scourge upon the citizenry and were run out of town. Yet, today in modern times, the cult of "Doctor Worship" is alive and well and has become the societal norm among a people who reject the counsel of God and instead believe the twisted contrivances of corrupt men. Enslaved by the media-promoted falsehood indoctrinations of the diabolical Medical Criminal Fraternity, the general public has been made hopelessly dependent upon a healthcare scam that maintains them in a condition of ill-health and vunerability to chronic diseases. No cures are ever forthcoming; no remedies are allowed by the corrupt AMA. Alternative means to circumvent the satanic medical system are supressed, scorned, blacklisted, and deemed illegal by the globalist's FDA.

The final word about the Medical Crime Cartel is that, if you wish to be free of illness and disease, and live to the full potential of your years in perfect health, stay away from doctors!

THE MEDICAL CRIMINAL FRATERNITY

For decades you have believed the lies of organized medicine. Once you start to realize that the medical profession is a detriment to your health, you will perhaps understand they are operating with an agenda passed on to them from the Hierarchy of Illuminati globalists whose objective is to depopulate the world and maim or kill as many people as posssible. They are not looking for cures; they are looking for deaths.

The vaccine protocol is a major component of the Globalist's Agenda, and in basic design is comprehensive in geopolitical scope, with no tolerance for allowing anyone to escape from its prevasive outreach. So strigent are the government-mandated requirements to inoculate every warm human body on the face of the earth, that new born infants delivered in a hospital are snatched from a mother's loving arms, and the minute-old baby is injected with some of the most neurotoxic elements known to man. (One of those injections is for Hepatitis B, which only afflicts prostitutes and IV drug users, not infants.) This is the first round of biowarfare assaults upon the individual, and sets the stage for subsequent injections—sometimes as many as eight during a single office visit—that have been calculated to render the growing child physically and cognitively compromised, or dead. Mass death is integral to the globalist's depopulation agenda, and spreading as much disease and destruction among the human population is their top priority. *Vaccines,* perpetrated through the Medical Criminal Fraternity of doctors, pharmaceutical companies, hospitals and health clinics, are the globalist's primary vehicle for accomplishing that goal.

Since the inception of the vaccine campaign during the 1940's, the stakes have escalated in terms of human control and the detrimental consequences of vaccinations. (The earliest mandatory vaccine was the polio vaccine, and nearly all cases of polio can be attributed to the vaccine.) More recently, since 2020, nano-size microchips have been added to the death shot concoction. These are not typical silicon-based microchips, since they are fused with foreign DNA to create gene-splicing capability. Once human genes have been deleted and nonhuman genetic material has been inserted into chromosomes, the molecular reproductive machinery produces a new, never before seen copy of each cell. From the point at which genetic material has undergone that transcription, in the crossing-over process, an unique nonhuman cell has been replicated, and all the trillions of somatic and sex cells suffer the same biochip fate. Therefore, the ultimate goal of vaccines can be discerned: change the image of man from a God-likeness to a Satan-likeness, a man-made version of humanity, one with nonhuman genetics, without a Free Will or a God-fearing Soul.

The global elite's stated objective is to create a new species upon the planet, a cyborg robotized microchipped (by Covid and other vaccine injections) transhuman that is reproductively sterile and under their complete control. Vaccine microchipping and gene splicing will enable them to achieve that goal.

Only the exercise of your Free Will can deny them access to your body and prevent them from destroying your health and commandeering your future destiny. Loss of personal Salvation is the ultimate consequence of being injected with the 666 Covid vaccine or any of its subsequent "Variants" (Revelation 14:9–11).

THE GLOBALISTS WILL USE FOOD AS A WEAPON

There exists a real and present danger to your health by indiscriminately consuming food items offered on the shelves of your local grocery store. More than 98 percent of those items are detrimental to your physical and mental integrity, and in many instances are lethal for a continuance of your longevity. Thus, food selection is of utmost importance for every discerning person, and especially in regard to their newborn infants and young children, who are in various stages of forming Central Nerveous System neural connections. Much of the physiological damage which manifests as illness or disease later on in adult life was initiated prenatally in the mother's womb, or during the time of infancy and throughout the childhood years as a consequence of vaccines and genetically engineered weaponized processed packaged food obtained from supermarkets and restaurants. In nearly all cases, the causal factor was either dietary intake or vaccines.

FOOD PRODUCTS THAT ARE UNSAFE TO CONSUME

The packaged foods which are readily available at the supermarket have nearly all been laced with toxic chemical components and contain ingredients which have undergone genetic modification in a deliberate attempt to cause illness and disease among an undiscerning public. Food labeling laws do not provide warning of this danger, and the typical consumer is left without any basis for evaluating the safety of the food and beverage items they take home to feed their family.

Very few people realize the relationship which exists between diet and health and the impact their food selection has upon their general state of physical and psychological well-being. Most were raised in a culture where McDonald's, Burger King, and Taco Bell were considered to be sources of food, never realizing that the entire agricultural, food processing, packaging and distribution industry is controlled at the top by the multi-trillion dollar crime families of the world, whose Agenda is depopulation and to maintain the global populous in a state of abject ill health and health-related ingnorance, while supplying synthetic food facsimiles that look and taste good but are counterproductive to sustaining life. Food producers have no motivation or concern in regard to nutritional benefits, but only for packaging attractive food products with an infinite shelf life for increasing profits. There is little chance for the uninformed to escape from the conspiratorial clutches of the Luciferian madmen generating massive cash flow from proliferating sickness and disease, and from engendering a toxic chemical dependency among those uneducated in matters of food selection and the impact their choices have upon their physical and mental state.

Alternative healthcare enterprises typically focus upon the profit motive when presenting a new packaged "wonder food" or ingredient that is believed to provide healthful benefits. Yet, they lack understanding about the misconceptions and dangers of isolating constituents of whole foods and concentrating them as a curative elixir. Naive enough to believe the hype, they will subsequently create a nutrient imbalance with biochemical side effects resulting from not having ingested the whole food in its natural state. The complex of biochemical processes are only in balance when all the necessary nutrient components—*in exactly the correct proportions*—are present in the foods that are consumed. There is only one way to insure that balance, and it is a strict adherence to the Genesis 1:29 Diet (ref. Book: *Genesis 1:29 Diet*).

Achieving dietary balance for maintaining a healthy body and sound mind is accomplished by identifying which commercial food products to avoid, and which to incorporate as the sole unadulterated foods that comprise your daily diet. Your response to the FDA's effort to render your food unfit for humans is a knowledge of which food products and beverages are safe, and which are not safe for human consumption.

GENESIS 1:29 DIET

Let's begin at the beginning, with God and his 1611 King James Bible; the Creator of the universe, knowing all there is to be known. We find the first human essentially strolling around in a fruit orchard jungle-type environment, and God Almighty declares, in a single verse of Scripture, what constitutes the proper diet for a human being. Here it is—in just one powerful sentence—what should be the entirety of one's everyday food intake: *And God said, Behold, I have given you every herb bearing seed, which is upon the face of all the earth, and every tree, in the which is the fruit of a tree yielding seed; to you it shall be for meat* (Genesis 1:29). Note that there is no reference in this passage to packaged processed synthetic foods or bottled beverages. There is no mention of feeding neurotoxic MSG and Aspartame-poisoned breakfast cereals to your innocent little children. This verse does not speak of Monsanto genetically-altered processed food facsimiles, soy-based products, carcinogenic packaged food products, or neurosynapse-destroying fluoridated tap water. No where in that verse does it state anything about consuming animal carcasses. In fact, it implies that nothing needs to die for the sake of your sustenance. Just pick your dinner off a tree or pull it out of the ground.

There were no restaurants in the Garden of Eden; no greasy spoon family diners, no over-priced eating establishments where you indulge now and pay dearly for it later. There were only fruit-bearing trees—lots of them, and every kind imaginable—not only the proverbial apple, but also the full spectrum of citrus: oranges, grapefruit, lemons, etc; and pears, bananas, cherries, peaches, figs, pomegranates, etc; and nut-yielding trees: almond, pecan, walnut, etc. And growing out of the ground were grape-yielding vines, and the grains: wheat, oats, rice, barley, and other Mediterranean species, including some that are likely to be extinct today. Also, the seeds of plants: sunflower, pumpkin, sesame, etc. Everything was organic, no pesticides were used, no genetic modification. It was dietary perfection, real food that was never touched by the wickedness of man. The Garden was truly a paradise, with beautiful birds singing in the trees and a multitude of four-footed creatures that did not have to worry about a sudden bullet or a piercing arrow; the excruciating pain of a cruel demise at the hand of some psychologically unbalanced stalker or agribusiness pursuing them to their death while systematically killing off millions yearly to feed a perverse craving for sinking their teeth into an animal carcass. Living a brief life of constant fear, the indignity, trauma and profound sense of loss from witnessing the death of a life-long familiar companion, and the vague realization that they would be next, is all the future they would ever know. The day would surely come when the exploited beautiful creature would become merely a lifeless stripped body in a slaughter house; an unmoving bloody dead corpse hanging on a hook, a cut up piece of plastic-wrapped meat in a supermarket display case.

So, we see that man fell, in the Garden, and disobeying God, would forever walk in fear and apprehension of the source of his next meal, never conscious of the world from which he had his origin. There was no looking back from there, and he forgot what it was like to be in fellowship with his Creator, to listen to the voice of God. He lost the ability to hear from the Eternal, to know his Word. When man transgressed the Laws of God his communication was severed, and his involvement in the mass of humanity reinforced his disbelief. All that remained was to be preyed upon by the liars for profit; the proud, "wearing no beautiful robe," and with the initials "M.D." after their gold monogramed name. Man became a prisoner of his ignorance, devoid of the knowledge of God; and standing for nothing, fell for everything. Thinking themselves wise, they became fools who could not recognize the truth. They hated knowledge; they trusted in their warped perceptions and despised the Source of all wisdom. For that, they received recompense in the form of frequent illnesses, chronic diseases, premature aging, and a shortened lifespan. If only they had believed God and obeyed his commandment not to eat of the "tree" that would be the cause of their destruction. If only they had become as they were "In the beginning. . ."

The top limit of human longevity was the first man, Adam, 930 years. In the eighth generation, Methuselah lived to 969 years. By the tenth generation the life span shortened to 590 years (Noah), but not everyone lived a long life during that first 10 generations. Some died at 100 years and even 70 years. By the era of Moses, about 2000 years later, he lived to be 120 years, considered an old man at that time, but remained strong and healthy until his last day. A thousand years subsequent to that time (1000 BC), during the reign of King David, the life span was 70–80 years, which is what it is today. (It fluctuated lower, reaching the lowest level during 300AD, when the lifespan was about 35 years, but that was due to wars, plagues, and harsh living conditions.)

In modern times, a higher percentage of people are living to the ages of 70–80, and some into their 90's, but their physical and psychological health is marginal and their quality of life is reduced as they are continually preyed upon by the "for profit" Medical Crime Cartel planned eugenic culling of the elderly.

Scripture regarding human longevity (Psalm 90:10):

The days of our years are threescore years and ten; and if by reason of strength they be fourscore years, yet is their strength labour and sorrow; for it is soon cut off, and we fly away. Three score and ten is 70; fourscore is 80. So, the best that can be done is to live 70 very healthy years, and then diminished health throughout the 70–80 period. It is possible to be healthy during those last 10 years, but probably not as vibrant as during the period up to 70. Certainly, any contact with, or dependance upon, the Medical Criminal Fraternity will expedite physical and mental decline with advancing years.

Yet, there is still a "wild card" to longevity, and it is to be found in this verse of Scripture: *Who satisfieth thy mouth with good things; so that thy youth is renewed like the eagle's* (Psalm 103:5). The "good things" referred to in this verse is the Genesis 1:29 Diet. The rest of the verse can only be understood in terms of the context from which it was derived: An eagle in the wild may live 60 years, and then must shed it's claws, beak, and molt its feathers in order to renew its strength and live nearly twice as long with renewed vigor. Likewise, a human being may be granted a second chance at life. (The parallel is to be "Born Again.")

The Genesis 1:29 Diet is the same diet which the early generations of man subsisted upon during the "primative" stages of developing a "civilized" culture. People lived longer because there were no harmful environmental stress factors such as pollution, radiation, and weaponized food and drink. They fed their body with foods that God provided, not the perverse synthetic frankenfoods of today. Modern man is often sick and dies prematurely, and one of the primary causes is food products corrupted by the hand of wicked men.

In the modern world, 98 percent of all the many hundreds of packaged processed foods and beverages sold commercially are a source for acquiring degenerative diseases. With few exceptions, what may appear to be palliable food is actually a weaponized means for sabotaging your health. Fancy colorful packaging is designed to attract your attention and induce you to buy a product; a well-planned marketing strategy was deployed to out-compete other similar products vying for space on the supermarket shelves. When a food manufacturer formulates a lethal food or beverage there is no thought given for the consumer's health, but only a concern for generating a profit. The corrupt FDA does nothing to protect the public from the lethality of synthetic food derrivatives because they are under orders from their globalist masters to destroy the health of the world population—the Globalist's Agenda campaign is to depopulate (kill people), not promote good health and longevity. The resultant sickness and decline of the end user is never at issue; all effort has been focused on merchantiseability and shelf life of food facimilies that may look and taste sumptuous, but wreak havoc upon human physiology. As a globalist organization peopled by pharmaceutical drug company personnel, the FDA gives tacit authorization for insuring death and disease among the general population by granting approval to foods and beverages that contain chemical components and additives that are widely known to be carcinogenic, and while at the same time disallowing claims of naturally-occurring untainted foods essential and beneficial to human health. Neurotoxic substances such as Monosodium glutamate (MSG), Aspartame, genetically modified ingredients, and Fluoride are deemed acceptable by a criminal government institution entrusted with overseeing, regulating, and safeguarding the health of the American people. Virtually nothing is prohibited from entering the commercial food supply; almost everything is permissible if it has the potential to compromise health. Pure foods known for centuries to enhance physical and cognitive integrity are prohibited from making truthful health claims of curing illness and disease.

The food industry is closely regulated by globalist oversight; directives are sent down from the pinnacle of world control and carried out by food producers and individuals in high positions of government and biotechnology companies compromised by a genocidal Agenda and financial interest. (Most FDA officials are on the Board of Directors of pharmaceutical companies which produce food additives and vaccines.) Toxic synthetic foods and beverages are the ultimate consequence of an unholy alliance between big government, big pharma, and big agribusiness. Food labeling provides very little information for making healthy choices, and never warns of the associated risks from ingesting packaged processed food products. Health authorities are not subject to third party review, and rule from a position granted to them by the genocidal Medical Crime Cartel.

Reading ingredient labels will sometimes provide a list of added chemical substances and genetically modified (GM) components, but often those items are either not listed or mislabeled with an innocuous name. For example, there are over 50 names for MSG and

Aspartame, which are known neurotoxins. ("Natural Flavoring" is an FDA approved name for MSG, and is listed on the packaging of many food products.) Essentially, everything that has been added to the packaging contents has potential as a causal factor for acquiring illness or disease.

The following partial list of packaged processed foods do not promote good health and are thus unsafe for human consumption. Generally, they include nearly all the food items from the central isles at your local grocery store or suburban supermarket.

- Cooking oils, except grapeseed, coconut, olive, sunflower, are unsafe and should be avoided. Especially dangerous are canola, soybean, corn, rice bran, and cottonseed oils.

- Foods made from soybeans (99 percent of all soybeans produced in the U.S. have been genetically modified. America is the world's leading producer and exporter of soybeans.) This includes soy-based infant formulas, Tofu, protein powders and drinks, and ingredients present in many other products used for cooking and baking.

- All canned products. The ingredients are usually toxic, and the metals from the can may leach into the food. (The acid from tomatoes and sauces made from tomatoes reacts with the canned metal to form a gastric toxin.)

- All meat-containing products (cuts of various types of animals, sausage, etc.)

- All boxed, packaged, processed breakfast cereals.

- All breads, except for sprouted grain breads. (Look in the freezer department; brand name: "Food For Life.")

- All cake mixes, cookies and candies.

- Dairy products, including cow's milk, cheese, butter, and yogurt. (Except powdered goat milk, organic yogurt, and organic butter.)

- All bottled or package beverages and soft drinks.

This is only a partial list and can be added to for inclusion in the list of Unsafe Food items.

Food products prepared in a restaurant, or otherwise without your supervision or direction, are to be avoided. It is not possible to know with certainty the source, composition, or combination of ingredients that were used to create the synthetic amalgamation. Regardless of the assurance of the food provider, you can never be 100 percent certain that the prepared food is safe and without anything added that is detrimental to your health. There is nothing offered by restaurants that you cannot make for yourself at home, in your own kitchen, and at a much lower cost. If convenience is a consideration in your decision to expose yourself to a health risk, then you are either not fully aware of the dangers or do not sufficiently value your health to protect it from the many who only wish to make a profit. Your health is of no concern to those who operate a business enterprise; their Bottom Line is enhanced at the expense of your good health.

FOODS AND BEVERAGES THAT ARE SAFE FOR HUMAN CONSUMPTION

A basic knowledge of natural food sources and their nutrient composition is essential in order to identify health-promoting foods from non-foods that will compromise your health. Your objective should be to only focus upon whole fruits, whole vegetables, whole grains, nuts and seeds, and a few other natural food items such as honey, goat milk (powdered and reconstituted with distilled water), and all the various herbs, some of which are mentioned in the Bible. These naturally-occurring foods are Scripturally-approved by God to uniquely satisfy the nutritional needs of a human being. Limiting your food intake exclusively to these items will result in a state of sound health and freedom from illness and disease.

Essentially, your supermarket food selection should be restricted to the periphery of the store, avoiding the rows of long isles toward the middle of the room, and which contain hundreds of processed packaged non-food ingredients that will severely impair your health. The area where you will concentrate nearly all of your time whenever shopping for your weekly groceries is the fresh fruit and vegetable department. There you will find a large assortment of naturally-occurring unprocessed whole fruits, vegetables, nuts and various seeds (e.g. sunflower seeds, pumpkin seeds), that you can select from and buy in bulk for preserving by refrigeration to maintain freshness and nutrient content. The only caution is to avoid those whole foods which have been genetically modified or sprayed with pesticides. As previously mentioned, genetic modification alters the food item at the cellular level, and once consumed, will adversely affect physiological processes of your organs and bodily tissues. Also, there is an increasing potential for foods to contain genetic machinery to gene-splice foreign DNA sequences into your chromosomes (nanorobots are small enough to be added to processed foods and beverages), and the introduction of a long list of delayed-onset diseases such as various types of cancer; digestive disorders such as constipation, diarrhea, heartburn; and metabolic dysfunctions like Diabetes. While pesticides are lethal to invading insects in the field, when sprayed onto your fruits and vegetables they have a persistent residual effect which makes it difficult or impossible to remove by washing off chemical traces of the poison. It may also penetrate through a thin peel and be absorbed into the edible portion of the food. (Organic pesticides are no less toxic than petroleum-based non-organic pesticides because they chemically break down faster and wash off in the rain, and thus require twice the frequency of toxic spraying.)

When you consume only Genesis 1:29 naturally-occurring foods, and eliminate all pharmaceutal drugs from your diet, you will immediately notice a positive difference in your overall health and sense of well-being, as reflected by the way you look and feel; you will lose weight, seem lighter and enjoy ease of bodily movements; you will have more energy, and you will experience a sense of calm and renewed hope with each new day. Your mind will become clearer, problems will no longer seem as difficult, and your general outlook will show improvement. In a short period of time all your internal organs will begin to function perfectly, your joints will no longer ache, your blood pressure will drop to normal levels, heart beat will stabilize and grow stronger and more efficient; your arteries will open, as accumulated calcified deposits vanish; the oxygen penetration in your somatic tissue will increase to nearly 100 percent. All this, and much more, when you banish doctors, hospitals, and pharmaceutical drugs from your life by changing your diet from the death-promoting foods offered by a sick and decadent culture, to a diet that is specifically designed by God to meet the nutritional needs of a human being. Within 30 days of making this life-changing decision, you will have formed a habit, and it will become second nature for you to make the right food choices. That tendency to make good choices will carry over into other areas of your life, for you will now be seeking the perfect will of God, rather than the wicked counsel of man.

The Word of God establishes precedent:

Daniel 1:8,12–20: *But Daniel purposed in his heart that he would not defile himself with the portion of the king's meat, nor with the wine which he drank: therefore he requested of the prince of the eunuchs that he might not defile himself. . . . Prove thy servants, I beseech thee, ten days; and let them give us* pulse *to eat, and* water *to drink. Then let our countenances be looked upon before thee, and the countenance of the children that eat of the portion of the king's meat: and as thou seest, deal with thy servants. So he consented to them in this matter, and proved them ten days. And at the end of ten days their countenances appeared fairer and fatter in flesh than all the children which did eat the portion of the king's meat. Thus Melzar took away the portion of their meat, and the wine that they should drink; and gave them* pulse*. . . . As for these four children, God gave them knowledge and skill in all learning and wisdom: and Daniel had understanding in all visions and dreams. Now at the end of the days that the king had said he should bring them in, then the prince of the eunuchs brought them in before Nebuchadnezzar. And the king communed with them; and among them all was found* *none like Daniel, Hananiah, Mishael, and Azariah: therefore stood they before the king. And in all matters of wisdom and understanding, that the king enquired of them, he found them ten times better than all the magicians and astrologers that were in all his realm.*

"Pulse" is fruits and vegetables, the Genesis 1:29 Diet. *"Water"* is pure water in the form of steam distilled. All other methods of purification (e.g. filtration) are inferior quality, with contaminates.

Condition yourself to not follow the crowd; find out what everybody else does, then do the exact opposite. Obey God, and you will be healthy until your last day of occupying a physical body. As long as you continue in the ways of the Almighty God Jesus Christ, you will experience his blessings for your obedience to his Word. You shall be physically, mentally, and spiritually in tune with your Creator, and will have in the process eliminated all of the health problems which frequently plague mankind. If you live with an eternal perspective, you shall truly live forever!

Summary of select Genesis 1:29 Foods that are safe to consume and are beneficial to your health

The following can be consumed in any quantity and often as you wish:

✓ Whole produce: wide variety of fruits, vegetables

✓ Nuts, seeds

✓ Honey

✓ Whole grain products: breads, pastas, noodles, wheat germ, etc. (Recommended Brand name of sprouted bread: Food For Life)

✓ Goat Milk: powdered form (Recommended Brand: Meyenberg), reconstituted with water purified by Steam Distillation

✓ Yogurt (Organic, Plain)

✓ Homemade, fresh squeezed or blended fruit juices: Lemon water is a systemic disinfectant. Dilute one squeezed lemon per 12 oz glass of Distilled Water. (Drink through a straw; tooth contact with the high acid content erodes enamel.)

✓ Drink no other beverages except Distilled water

**A review of counterproductive health practices—What NOT to do
Do not:**

- Get vaccinated

- Drink alcohol or take legal or illegal drugs

- Feed your infants or children any foods or beverages formulated for infants or children

- Consume soy or corn, or soy-based or corn-based food products

- Consume anything made with these oils: Palm, Canola, Cottonseed, Soybean, Safflower, Corn, Rice bran, Margarine (or any "buttery spread")

- Dine in restaurants

- Consume packaged processed foods or beverages

- Drink municipal tap water

- Take vitamin and mineral supplements, or any kind of packaged processed concentrated nutrients, powders, pills, or formulations

ADDITIONAL KEY POINTS

All citrus naturally-occurring fruits contain Collagen-forming Hyluronic Acid, which is an essential component of the cellular matrix that maintains the integrity of the skin integument, facia, and fiberous connective tissue throughout the body. Tendons, ligaments, arteries and cell membranes require Collagen. Hyluronic Acid from naturally-occurring citrus Vitamin C sources (not from commercial skin care products, prescriptions, pills, capsules or tablet Supplements) confers a cell-protective function and acts to rejuvenate skin and tighten the underlying tissue matrix. Skin will maintain or recover elasticity to enhance youthful appearance; it also promotes the integrity of all other tissues and organs. Insufficient Vitamin C in the diet will cause many types of illnesses, diseases, bacterial infections, and premature aging. This vitamin is water-soluble and is not stored in body organs; it is not synthesized and therefore must be supplied daily. Adult daily dosage: the equvalent of 5–10 medium sized oranges (350–700 mg). Children: 3–7 medium-sized oranges (210–490 mg), depending upon age. One medium-sized orange contains about 70 mg of Vitamin C. The minimum daily requirement for this vitamin is 200 mg; disinformation states that it is 100 mg. Ignore the lowered figure, since the controllers do not want you to know of this vitally important health benefit derived from ingesting an adequate quantity of whole citrus.

The Bible states that bread will strengthen your heart (Psalm 104:15). Only purchase whole grain breads that are certified organic and non-GMO free of genetic modification. Sprouted-grain breads contain nutrients that are better assimulated and bioavailabile. This will improve cardiac status for sustaining a strong and healthy cardiovascular system.

Prostrate cancer is common today among middle-age and elderly men, and is lethal. Regularly consuming Pumpkin Seeds will combat this disease and neutralize the formation of this type of cancer.

Dental health is an indicator for over-all health. Gingivitis and Peridontal disease can be avoided by observing the Genesis 1:29 Diet, which is free of refined sugar, and by swishing a salt water solution in your mouth every night before retiring. Himalayan pink salt is recommended; Distilled Water is essential.

The quality of Steam Distilled Water will vary, depending upon the source. When purchased in 1 gallon plastic jugs from the supermarket, the low-grade plastic leaches into the water and is toxic. Counter top distillation units are made with plastic components and other materials which contaminate the purified water. There are only two other possibilities for obtaining pure water: (1): Purchase it in 5 gallon bottles from a producer of Distilled Water, (2): Buy your own electric distiller from a manufacturer and purify your own water. The unit must be high-grade stainless steel and have an output capacity of at least one gallon of distilled water per hour. Overpriced and inefficient American-made units are not recommened; obtain from overseas. China has several brands that are industrial grade, high output and level of purity, and at a substantially lower cost (approx. $200, plus $200 shipping).

Use only heat-resistant tempered glass cooking vessels; Vision-ware, Lennox, etc., obtainable Online from Ebay, Amazon. No longer available in stores. (Because organic brain disease is not transmitted by glass cook ware.) Never use metal pots and pans for cooking, and especially those made from Aluminum.

The Pineal Gland is the control center for regulating all the other endocrine glands in the body. It requires the amino acid Arginine to properly function. Nuts, especially almonds, contain a high percent-age of Arginine. Enhanced brain function is one of the benefits of consuming Fatty Acid nuts and seeds.

Certain Genesis 1:29 foods, such as cherries, grapes, berries (blueberries, blackberries, cranberries, elderberries), contain anti-oxidants and the nutrient Anthrocyanin which expands the lumen of the capillary micro-circulation in the brain to allow for increased blood flow that enables brain tissue to be more fully oxygenated. This is important for the prevention of neurological diseases like Parkin-son's and Alzheimer's.

Chelation is a process of extracting toxic elements from the brain and other organs. Chelating agents bind with the damaging heavy metal and remove it from the body. Examples of such agents are: Chlorella algae and Cilantro parsely, used in combination. Chlo-rella crosses the blood-brain barrier and binds with toxins; Cilantro removes it from the body. Other naturally-occurring sources are: Ascorbic acid (from whole citrus), Distilled water, uncooked Garlic and Onions, Lemon water, Gluthathione, Saffron, etc. (Do not use any pharmaceutical Drug Chelating Agents.) Chelation can improve or cure Autism. For each unit of Mercury, Aluminum, Lead or other toxins removed from a child's brain, there will be a corresponding reduction in the symptoms of Autism and learning disabilities.

The seeds within fruits are medicinal. They contain a form of Cyanide which is lethal to cancer cells, yet, is not toxic to humans. The seed of such fruits as Lemon, Orange, Avocado, etc., are potent sources of an effective means to cure all forms of Cancer. Read the Genesis 1:29 Scripture to ascertain the subtility of an all-knowing God who implies that the seeds of fruit are essential for maintaining good health: . . . *and every tree, in the which is the fruit of a tree yielding seed* . . . Why did God mention the seeds? Because in the seed there exists power to regenerate new life, to re-create and restore that which has died. (Inside the seed husk is a smaller seed. That is what should be eaten.)

The author's Pro-Antibiotic Diet consists of the following (from whole foods, not supplements):

✓ Citrus (Vitamin C/Ascorbic acid)

✓ Garlic & Onions (Sulfur)

✓ Nuts, Seeds, Grains (Zinc and Selenium)

✓ Salt (Himalayian Pink Salt; teaspoon in 8 oz glass of distilled water)

✓ Sunshine (Vitamin D3)

The minerals contained in the salt (e.g. Magnesium) are catalysts for activating the vitamins and other nutrients in the food to enable their bioavailability. Consume all of the above during the course of a meal; no need to premix. The ultraviolet rays of the Sun activate the immune system and destroy pathogens throughout the body.

The best storage foods are:

- Canned tuna (in water, not oil): A 4 oz can contains 30 grams of protein, which is more than half the daily requirement for adults; plus vital nutrients. The cost is about $1–$2, which could sustain life for a day.

- Nuts (for energy): High protein, good source of vitamins and minerals; fatty acids preferred by the brain. Peanuts in the shell only. Do not trust any packaged shelled nuts or peanut butters, since the peanut oil (or other healthy oil) has been replaced with GM oil, usually Canola (cheapest and most deadly), in order to increase profits by selling the good oil. The substituted GM oil is not listed on the ingredients label . . . and the globalist's complicit FDA does nothing about it.

- Seeds (minerals): No canola oil, cottonseed oil, safflower oil, palm oil, soybean oil, corn oil. Only peanut oil, sunflower oil, olive oil, grapeseed oil, coconut oil.

- Fruits and vegetables: Key fruit is citrus: oranges, grapefruit (red), kiwi, etc. Therefore, best to locate near a commercial fruit orchard—pick them off the trees, or otherwise buy in bulk and preserve by temperature control (refrigerator or low temperature outdoor environment). When on the run, too bulky and heavy to carry around with you, so need a cache somewhere remote.

- Powdered goat milk: Walmart, $11.95. Will last 2–4 weeks for one person. Just mix with distilled water. Essentially a complete food in itself. When consumed with the above items your diet will be balanced and you will be healthy, without any illness or disease.

Genetically Modified Oils are one of the more insidious aspects of the globalist's depopulation Agenda. GM Vegetable cooking oils are the principal cause of digestive disorders like Colitus, and lethal metabolic diseases such as Diabetes, as well as many "incurable" unrelated chronic ailments, including heart disease. (A protruding abdomen and resistant excess fat at the midsection is nearly always an indication of GM oils in one's diet.) Consumption of any processed food products made with or containing GM oils will impede the gastric breakdown of carbohydrates, fats and proteins, and will inhibit nutrient uptake by the intestial villa. (After a meal you feel "bloated" and as if there is "a brick" in your stomach. You may still be hungry, but cannot eat any more . . . you have been poisoned by the genetically modified oils in your food.) Many types of degenerative diseases are linked to the consumption of GM oils as the precipitating factor. Maladies include: resistant obesity, tissue endema, compromised immunological response; joint stiffness and pain, cartilage deterioation, and other autoimmune diseases.

Globalist-controlled food manufacturers replace healthy oils, such as grapeseed, sunflower, oilve, coconut, peanut, with one or more GM oils that will cause serious illness and life-long diseases.

The following deadly oils are present in nearly all processed package foods: Canola (GM rapeseed), palm, soybean, cottonseed, corn, safflower, and others. Canola is used in certain parts of the world as a machinary lubricant, and was further modified to "lubricate" humans for the expressed purpose of inducing illness and premature death. All restaurants, including "health food" restraurants, use this lethal oil because of its low cost and availability. (This inducement is by globalist design.)

DONALD TRUMP:
A PORTRAIT OF COMPROMISE

What impressed this author the most about Donald J. Trump is that he was and continues to be the object of intense division among the American people, and that was of a polarizing extremity seldom seen in U.S. politics. The reigning President of the most powerful nation in history was ostensibly in a position that could significantly impact America and the entire world.

Throughout his term, the residing Chief Executive was targeted by a horde of enemies that pursued him with concerted fervor; they opposed him on nearly every issue and rose up against his many decrees to prevent good from prevailing against their evil. Yet, a closer look at the man reveals he was compromised by Illuminati interests, and was a pivotal transition for bringing in the Covid fake pandemic.

The truth regarding the deposed President can best be seen by how he acted in response to three key issues: Immigration, Voter Fraud, and Personal Identification. He proposed an "RFID Visa Tracking System" to prevent illegal immigration, argued the need for photo-verified "Voter ID," and promised that as President he would insist on "ID to purchase anything." He believed that service should be refused to anyone who did not submit to a photo identification means of ID verification. He was also supportive of propaganda furthering the Covid lie. Most significantly, he was in agreement with the globalist's design for a digital human-branding system that would number, surveillance, and track everyone on the planet. Therefore, Trump was one of "Them" and would betray the American people and the entire world under the pretense of "Be Safe."

During the latter part of his term, Trump announced before a crowd of his supporters that shoppers need to show photo identification in order to buy groceries. http://www.youtube.com/ watch?v=W4cCeiccSzU He pushed for stricter voting laws and claimed that photo identification should always be required. He said,"Only American citizens should vote in American elections, which is why the time has come for voter ID . . . If you go out and you want to buy groceries, you need a picture on a card, you need ID. You go out and you want to buy anything, you need ID and you need your picture." This declaration is an incremental step toward the prophesied Mark of the Beast microchip/Luciferase tattoo. He was thus clearly complicit with globalist genocidal control.

Therefore, Trump compromised his integrity and was proven to be yet another Illuminati shill, controlled opposition which superficially appeared as the people's advocate, but who would capitulate to preserve his life and further the interests of his Rothschild masters. (This was predicted in the author's book, *The Coming of Wisdom,* published in 2016.) Behind the scenes, the duplicity runs deep.

Donald Trump was either naive or compromised, and was the classic controlled opposition. Ostensibly the people's advocate, he supported the Covid deception.

Biden is the overt form of the Illuminati's Hegelian Dialect, and would go on to do whatever was commanded by his Rothschild handlers. The mask is an outward indication of his submission to Satan; a compliant, senile, low IQ political puppet. (Blue-tinted skin indicates Hypoxia from lack of oxygen to his brain.)

FOR FURTHER STUDY

BOOKS:

George Orwell—Nineteen Eighty-Four

By Soul Esprit:
—The Criminal Fraternity
—The Globalist's Agenda
—When Will the Illuminati Crash the Stock Market?
—The Great Deception
—The Coming of Wisdom
—Seven Who Dared
—Genesis 1:29 Diet

By Forrest Maready:
—The Autism Vaccine
—Unvaccinated
—Crooked: Man-Made Disease Explained

ARTICLES & VIDEOS:

—Childrens Health Defense: COVID–19: The Spearpoint for

Rolling Out a "New Era" of High –Risk, Genetically Engineered Vaccines

—Compulsory Vaccination, the Constitution, and the Hepatitis B Mandate for Infants and Young Children by Mary Holland

—Hero of the Week: March 12, 2020—Former President Of Microsoft Canada, Frank Clegg

—Corbett Report: Bill Gates x 5

—Collection Cup: Building a List of Best Sources on Vaccine Risks

RELATED READING:

—Children's Health Defense

—VAXXED

—VAXXED II: The People's Truth

—Jon Rappoport at nomorefakenews.com

—Robert Kennedy, Jr., Vaccine injury Attorney

INFORMATION WEBSITES:

—HumansAreFree.com

—vaxxter.com

—drbuttar.com

—Children Health Defense

—The High Wire

—Informed Consent Action Network

—Libetycenter.org

—NationalLLibertyAlliance.org

RELEVANT TOPICS:

Identity Management in 2020

file:///C:/Users/Guest1/AppData/Local/Temp/MicrosoftEdge
Downloads/84197f33–3bc5–455d–8558–d5286efc03b5/Netherlands
–Paper%20Expert%20Meeting%20IdentityManagement2030%20
def–151109%20(1).pdf

Project: L.U.C.I.D.

https://www.google.com/search?q=Project:+L.U.C.I.D.–PDF&
source=lnms&tbm=isch&sa=X&ved=2ahUKEwjXxr3Pkd3tAhX
VrZ4KHe6mD5oQ_AUoAXoECAcQAw&biw=1536&bih=782

Switzerland: Digital I.D. by 2030

https://www.google.com/search?ei=O4nfX_W–JaKSoPEP_butw
AU&q=Switzerland%3A+Digital+I.D.+by+2030&oq=Switzer
land%3A+Digital+I.D.+by+2030&gs_lcp=CgZwc3ktYWIQAzoE
CAAQR1CZmWFY4OBhYML5YWgAcAJ4AIABeIgBoQWSAQM
3LjGYAQCgAQGqAQdnd3Mtd2l6yAEIwAEB&sclient=psy–ab
&ved=0ahUKEwi1yIeeit3tAhUiCTQIHf1dC1gQ4dUDCAo&uact=5

SB 362 Senate Bill

http://www.leginfo.ca.gov/pub/07–08/bill/sen/sb_0351–0400/sb
_362_bill_20071012_chaptered.html

Contact Tracing

https://www.google.com/search?q=Contact+Tracing&tbm=
isch&ved=2ahUKEwjAhMDzid3tAhUrATQIHV6bDx8Q2–cCeg
QIABAA&oq=Contact+Tracing&gs_lcp=CgNpbWcQAzIHCAA
QsQMMQQzIFCAAQsQMyAggAMgQIABBDMgIIADICCAAy
AggAMgIIADICCAAyAggAOgYIABAKEBg6BggAEAcQHjoI
CAAQBxAFEB46BggAEAUQHlDCPlipW2C5X2gAcAB4AIABW4g
BzQKSAQEomAEAoAEBqgELZ3dzLXdpei1pbWfAAQE&sclient
=img&ei=4ojfX8CLFquCoPEP3ra——AE&bih=782&biw=1536

The Great Reset
https://www.google.com/search?q=The+Great+Reset&source=
lnms&tbm=isch&sa=X&ved=2ahUKEwjBkvXhkd3tAhVNip4K
HSsbChUQ_AUoA3oECAkQBQ&biw=1536&bih=782&dpr=1.25

Text—H.R.6666—116th Congress (2019 –2020): COVID-19 Testing, Reaching, And Contacting Everyone (TRACE) Act | Congress.gov | Library of Congress
https://www.congress.gov/bill/116th-congress/house-bill/6666/
text?r=2&s=1

The Mark of the Beast?! 060606 A1—CryptoCurrency System Body Activity Data | The Daily Plane
https://www.thedailyplane.com/mark-of-beast-060606-crypto
currency-system-body-activity-data/

The Coronavirus COVID-19 Pandemic: The Real Danger is "Agenda ID2020"
What is the infamous ID2020? It is an alliance of public–private partners, including UN agencies and civil society. It's an electronic ID program that uses generalized vaccination as a platform for digital identity.
    https://www.globalresearch.ca/coronavirus-causes-effects
–real–danger–agenda–id2020/5706153

How to decondition yourself from social conditioning—Ste Davies
https://www.stedavies.com/decondition-yourself-from-social
–conditioning/

Social –Conditioning
https://www.google.com/search?q=Social-Conditioning&source
=lnms&tbm=isch&sa=X&ved=2ahUKEwixn7mIld3tAhV1HjQ
IHRYKCkEQ_AUoAnoECBwQBA&biw=1536&bih=782

Reaction to North Korea Requesting Vaccines While Having Zero Reported Cases—YouTube •Jan 6, 2021
https://www.youtube.com/watch?v=QAaKYmEfVPI

440 HZ Mind Control Druidic Frequency in Modern Music
https://www.youtube.com/watch?v=rTJVWCUpJEI&list=PL9Zuh M7Ca4UC4kpDS7Mige9HTSWZ –wMJo&index=189

Bill Gates has purchased 500,000 acres of farm land in 19 States for growing GM produce and GM farm animals
https://humansarefree.com/2021/01/why-is-bill-gates-buying-up -farmland-across-america.html

The Truth about Realty: You are a spirit living in a spirit-filled matrix
https://www.youtube.com/watch?v=omWY74exXZo

These 'vaccine hunters' are getting their shots ahead of schedule by gaming the system - CNN

Dodger Stadium mass vaccination site briefly shut down by anti-vaxxers this weekend, police say - CNN

Andrew Brooks, who led development of the first FDA-approved Covid-19 saliva test, dies at 51 - CNN

American jobs won't return to pre-pandemic levels until 2024, CBO says - CNN

The Ultimate Purpose of the Lockdowns: The Creation of a New Economic System Run by the Global Elite - Jamesjpn.net

The Injection Fraud—It's Not a Vaccine—Solari Report

How The Illuminati Want To Control You - David Icke - YouTube
https://www.google.com/search?q=Are+Human-Populations
+Being+Primed+For+Nano-Microchips+Inside+of+COVID-19
+Vaccines%3F!!%3A&oq=Are+Human-Populations+Being+Primed
+For+Nano-Microchips+Inside+of+COVID-19+Vaccines%3F!!%3A
&aqs=chrome..69i57&sourceid=chrome&ie=UTF-8

The 2020s: Things to Come - YouTube - https://www.youtube.com/
watch?v=rjNqLEhIkbc&pbjreload=101

David Dees (1957–2020) was a champion for the cause of exposing the
global manipulation of human perceptions. His political art satire survives as
an ongoing testimony to the truth he conveyed to a world enslaved by the
controlled media. His sudden unexpected demise occurred shortly after the
commencement of the Covid fake pandemic, suggesting that he was murdered (by directed pulsed ionizing radiation, inducing cancer) for exposing
falsehoods and diseminating the truth. His art form affected many lives and
increased public awareness to the reality of the Globalist's Agenda. (Some
of his powerful images were included in this book and were covers for other
books.)

CHEMTRAILS

It has become increasingly difficult to locate on the Internet any truthful reports regarding the reality and intention of Chemtrails. Nearly all Google searches of the term will produce pages of government disinformation targeting "Conspiracy Theory." Chemtrails are a $1 billion per day *global human-spray operation* to create an electro-magnetic atmospheric grid for transmitting HAARP microwave frequencies, propagating 5G mind-control electromagnetic radiation (.01–100 HZ), and to enable the Starlink/AI Neuralink between the human brain and Artificial Intelligence. Micronized particulate Aluminum and other metals present in the aerosol Chemtrail jet effluent cause upper respiratory diseases among the human population upon inhalation and absorption through the skin of the nano-sized toxic metals and bioengineered viral and bacterial pathogens (Upper Respiratory Disease is currently the third leading cause of death in America.) Uptake of Chemtrail nanoparticulate heavy metals in soil by plants and ingestion by humans and animals is an effective means for the globalists to create neurological diseases of unknown origin, and to make the human body an electromagnetic receiver of HAARP and Starlink/5G pulsed transmissions.

The prevalence of nano-particulate Aluminum in the lower atmosphere and upon the surface of the planet has serious medical consequences in terms of human cognitive function and overall physical health. Globally, the incidence of neurological diseases has spiked on statistical charts (#7) showing the increase in Alzheimer's, Parkinson's, and other acquired brain dysfunctions since the inception of the worldwide Chemtrail spray operation.

ARE CHEMTRAILS
A TRANSDIMENSIONAL INTERFACE?

As an integral aspect of the Globalist's Agenda, Chemtrails have a *spiritual* component and are an electronic medium for conducting HAARP microwave frequencies and Starlink 5G pulsed energy transmissions to the human brain. Although the clearly visible global sky campaign was begun in 1998 (23 years ago from the present date), few people are aware Chemtrails exist and will refuse to acknowledge the implications. Their ignorance and denial is because of the globalist's media suppression of the truth, and is also a result of the curse of Spiritual Blindness (2 Thess 2:10–12).

Chemtrails, in the form of a satanic pentagram image, was photographed directly above the author's house on the day he published his first book.

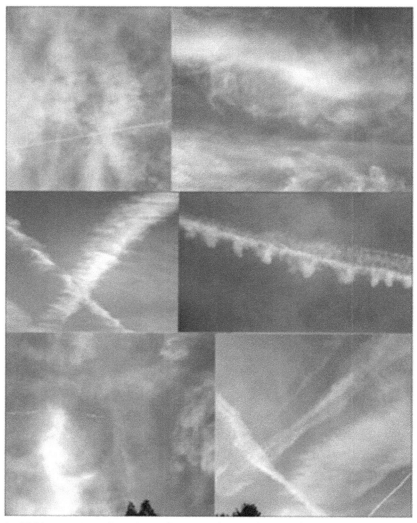

In 2011, a series of random photographs of Chemtrails were taken by the author and later revealed the above images. Detail of the top left and bottom left photos is shown below.

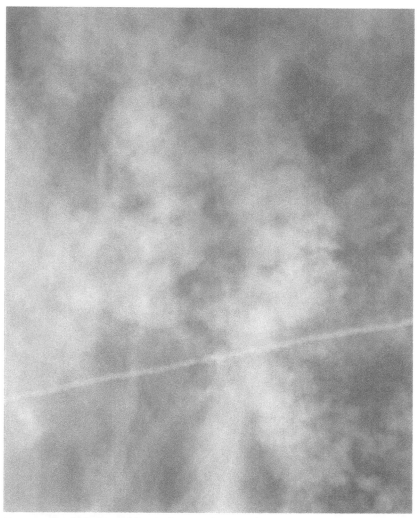

Unretouched photograph of Chemtrails reveals two faces conversing with each other. Could Chemtrails be a medium for the next higher dimension manifesting in the 3-dimensional material realm? Is it a spiritually-charged substrate with prophetic Biblical significance for the present End Times?

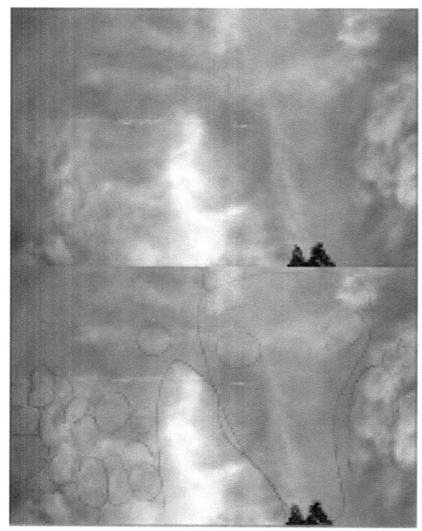

Circled images in the lower photograph show individual demonic faces. The central large bright figure is of someone seated; robed, laughing, sketched below. Can you guess who it is? *2 Corinthians 11:14: And no marvel; for Satan himself is transformed into an angel of light.*

The Globalist's Agenda is not a political agenda, it is a *Spiritual Agenda.*

THE GLOBALIST'S AGENDA
Companion book to THE GLOBALIST'S AGENDA END GAME
Hardcover: over 300 pages

In fiction and nonfiction works, Soul Esprit addresses a wide range of topics including political, medical, and religious corruption. The author of 12 books, he writes from both a spiritual and scientific perspective.

POSTSCRIPT

As this volume has predicted, there will be a worldwide citizen protest to the fake pandemic. Yet, the globalist's media is able to counter
by a continuous stream of disinformation to reinforce the Covid
massive delusion among the brainwashed masses. FEMA camps are
in place for incarceration of the escalating many who will gather in
protest and refuse to be vaccinated. ("Left-wing/Right-wing" paradigm is the Hegelian Dialectic: Problem-Reaction-Solution. It only
exists as a political tool to divide and conquer.)

Science Health News Germany: police clash with protesters against virus measures. Recent video link of worldwide protests of fake pandemic, quarantines,
business shutdowns, wearing of masks, social distancing, vaccinations:
https://153news.net/watch_video.php?v=67YK8DD5GO9Y

(1 of 11) Various initiatives and left-wing groups demonstrate against a demo of right-wing extremists and so-called "Reichsbuerger" in Berlin, Germany, Saturday, March 20, 2021. Right-wing extremists and "Reich citizens" are demonstrating around the Brandenburg Gate today. (Fabian Sommer/dpa via AP)

March 20, 2021

BERLIN (AP)—Protesters in Germany clashed with police Saturday over coronavirus measures, with officers using water cannons, pepper spray and batons against people trying to break through police barriers, German news agency dpa reported.

Protests against government measures to rein in the pandemic also were reported in several other European countries, including Austria, Switzerland and Finland. Around 10,000 people participated in the protest in the central German city of Kassel, where there also were confrontations between the demonstrators and counter-protesters.

Thousands of people marched through downtown Kassel despite a court ban, and most didn't comply with infection-control protocols such as wearing face masks. Some protesters attacked several journalists, dpa said.

Federal police, who were brought in beforehand from other parts of Germany, used water cannons and helicopters to control

the crowds, the news agency reported. Police said several people
were detained, but didn't give any numbers.

Various groups, most of them far-right opponents of government regulations to fight the pandemic, had called for protests
Saturday in cities across the country. Virus infections have gone
up again in Germany in recent weeks and the government is set
to decide next week on how to react.

Chancellor Angela Merkel said Friday Germany will have to
apply an "emergency brake" and reverse some recent relaxations
of restrictions as coronavirus infections accelerate. Germany's
national disease control center said new infections were growing exponentially as the more contagious COVID-19 variant first
detected in Britain has become dominant in the country.

On Saturday, the Robert Koch Institute reported 16,033 new
cases and registered 207 additional deaths, bringing the overall
death toll to 74,565 in Germany. In Berlin, some 1,800 police
officers were on standby for possible riots, but only about 500
protesters assembled at the city's landmark Brandenburg Gate.
Meanwhile, around 1,000 citizens came together on Berlin's
Unter den Linden boulevard to protest against the far-right

demonstration.

Police had to intervene when some far-right protesters tried to attack press photographers, but in general, a police spokeswoman told dpa, "there's not much going on here." In advance of the Berlin protests, authorities had announced they would create three special, police-protected areas where journalists could withdraw to when under attack by protesters, dpa reported. As in other countries, reporters are increasingly targeted during far-right demonstrations in Germany.

Protesters also hit the streets in other cities across Europe. In Finland, police estimated that about 400 people without masks and packed tightly together gathered in the capital, Helsinki, to protest government-imposed COVID-19 restrictions. Smaller demonstrations were scheduled in other Finnish cities.

Before the Helsinki rally, some 300 people chanting slogans like "Let the people speak!" and carrying placards with phrases such as "Facts and numbers don't add up" marched through the streets of the city, ending up at the Parliament building.

Helsinki police tweeted that the registered march and rally took place peacefully but violated social distancing requirements and Finland's current limits on public gatherings. Officers negotiated with event organizers to try to disperse the event.

An Associated Press reporter monitoring the action noted members of the pan-Nordic far-right group Soldiers of Odin attending the demonstration. In Austria, about 1,000 protesters participated in a demonstrations against the government's virus measures near Vienna's central train station. Police reprimanded several protesters who were not wearing masks and remaining too close together, news agency APA reported.

In Switzerland, more than 5,000 protesters met for a silent march in the community of Liestal 15 kilometers southeast of the city of Basel, local media reported. Most didn't wear masks and some held up banners with slogans like "Vaccinating kills."

OBEY GOD? OBEY SATAN?

Shadrach, Meshach, and Abednego would not bow down (submit) to the golden idol false god of the Babylonians when order by decree of the King of Babylon (circa 605 BC—562 BC). Consequently, he (the ruling government) commmanded them to be cast into a blazing furnace. Yet, they not only survived, but there was not even a trace of smoke on their garments. They refused to obey unrighteous authority, and God protected them.

This is only one Biblical example of God-ordained disobedience to unrighteous authority. What they did is the same as not bowing down to any unjust government law, ordinance, or mandate, including the wearing of a mask, social distancing, and receiving a vaccine. Trusting in God rather than men, by not submitting to an illegitimate authority **they steadfastly refused to support a lie, and God physically preserved them from certain death.**

If you commit to any of the fake pandemic acts of submission, you are in submission to Satan, whose religion is Human Civil Government, and your judgment shall follow—God will not preserve you in the globalist's firey furnace—and all the Revelation prophesy plagues will alight upon you.

Daniel 3:1–9; 12–14; 16–28:

Nebuchadnezzar the king made an image of gold, whose height was threescore cubits, and the breadth thereof six cubits: he set it up in the plain of Dura, in the province of Babylon. Then Nebuchadnezzar the king sent to gather together the princes, the governors, and the captains, the judges, the treasurers, the counsellors, the sheriffs, and all the rulers of the provinces, to come to the dedication of the image which Nebuchadnezzar the king had set up. Then the princes, the governors, and captains, the judges, the treasurers, the counsellors, the sheriffs, and all the rulers of the provinces, were gathered together unto the dedication of the image that Nebuchadnezzar the king had set up; and they stood before the image that Nebuchadnezzar had set up. Then an herald cried aloud, To you it is commanded, O people, nations, and languages, That at *what time ye hear the sound of the cornet, flute, harp, sackbut, psaltery, dulcimer, and all kinds of musick, ye fall down and worship the golden image that Nebuchadnezzar the king hath set up: And whoso falleth not down and worshippeth shall the same hour be cast into the midst of a burning fiery furnace. Therefore at that time, when all the people heard the sound of the cornet, flute, harp, sackbut, psaltery, and all kinds of musick, <u>all the people, the nations, and the languages, fell down and worshipped the golden image that Nebuchadnezzar the king had set up.</u> Wherefore at that time certain Chaldeans came near, and accused the Jews. They spake and said to the king Nebuchadnezzar, O king, live for ever. There are certain Jews whom thou hast set over the affairs of the province of Babylon, Shadrach, Meshach, and Abednego; these men, O king, have not regarded thee: they serve not thy gods, nor worship the golden image which thou hast set up. Then Nebuchadnezzar in his rage and fury commanded to bring Shadrach, Meshach, and Abednego. Then they brought these men before the king. Nebuchadnezzar spake and said unto them, Is it true, O Shadrach, Meshach, and Abednego, do not ye serve my gods, nor worship the golden image which I have set up? Shadrach, Meshach, and Abednego, answered and said to the king, O Nebuchadnezzar, <u>we are not careful to answer thee in this matter. If it be so, our God whom we serve is able to deliver us from the burning fiery furnace, and he will deliver us out of thine hand, O king. But if not, be it known unto thee, O king, that we will not serve thy gods, nor worship the golden image which thou hast set up.</u> Then was Nebuchadnezzar full of fury, and the form of his visage was changed against Shadrach, Meshach, and Abednego: therefore he spake, and commanded that they should heat the furnace one seven times more than it was wont to be heated. And he commanded the most mighty men that were in his army to bind Shadrach, Meshach, and Abednego, and to cast them into the burning fiery furnace. Then these men were bound in their coats, their hosen, and their hats, and their other garments, and were cast into the midst of the burning fiery furnace. Therefore because the king's commandment was urgent, and the furnace exceeding hot, the flames of the fire slew those men that took up Shadrach, Meshach, and Abednego.*

And these three men, Shadrach, Meshach, and Abednego, fell down bound into the midst of the burning fiery furnace. Then Nebuchadnezzar the king was astonished, and rose up in haste, and spake, and said unto his counsellors, Did not we cast three men bound into the midst of the fire? They answered and said unto the king, True, O king. He answered and said, Lo, I see four men loose, walking in the midst of the fire, and they have no hurt; and the form of the fourth is like the Son of God. Then Nebuchadnezzar came near to the mouth of the burning fiery furnace, and spake, and said, Shadrach, Meshach, and Abednego, ye servants of the most high God, come forth, and come hither. Then Shadrach, Meshach, and Abednego, came forth of the midst of the fire. And the princes, governors, and captains, and the king's counsellors, being gathered together, saw these men, upon whose bodies the fire had no power, nor was an hair of their head singed, neither were their coats changed, nor the smell of fire had passed on them. Then Nebuchadnezzar spake, and said, <u>Blessed be the God of Shadrach, Meshach, and Abednego, who hath sent his angel, and delivered his servants that trusted in him, and have changed the king's word, and yielded their bodies, that they might not serve nor worship any god, except their own God.</u>

. . . choose you this day whom ye will serve . . .
but as for me and my house, we will serve the Lord.
(Joshua 24:15)

What the Illuminati Globalists **FEAR** the most . . .

THE AUTHORIZED 1611 KING JAMES BIBLE IS THE ONLY WORD OF GOD.

There is one body, and one Spirit, even as ye are called in one hope of your calling; One Lord, one faith, one baptism, One God and Father of all . . .

(Ephesians 4:4–6).

There is Only ONE Word of God . . . Jesus Christ,

his name is called the Word of God (Revelation 19:13), *the way, the truth, and the life* (John 14:6), *the sword of the Spirit* (Ephesians 6:17), *quick, and powerful, and sharper than any twoedged sword* (Hebrews 4:12). *In the beginning was the Word, and the Word was with God, and the Word was God. The same was in the beginning with God. All things were made by him; and without him was not any thing made that was made. In him was life; and the life was the light of men. And the light shineth in darkness; and the darkness comprehended it not* (John 1:1–5).

Jesus Christ is God, One God, the *spoken* **Word of God**; His 1611 King James Bible is One Word, the *written* **Word of God**, Jesus Christ.

Sanctify them through thy truth: thy word is truth (John 17:17).

For I testify unto every man that heareth the words of the prophecy of this book, If any man shall add unto these things, God shall add unto him the plagues that are written in this book. And if any man shall take away from the words of the book of this prophecy, God shall take away his part out of the book of life, and out of the holy city, and from the things which are written in this book (Revelation 22:18,19).

Lightning Source UK Ltd.
Milton Keynes UK
UKHW021130270921
391259UK00011B/2308